WEAR YOUR
COLLAR

WEAR YOUR COLLAR

Gene Skipworth

Providence House Publishers

WWW.PROVIDENCEHOUSE.COM

FRANKLIN, TENNESSEE

Printed in the United States of America

14   13   12   11   10   1   2   3   4   5

Library of Congress Control Number: 2010923079

ISBN: 978-1-57736-440-5

Cover and page design by LeAnna Massingille

PROVIDENCE HOUSE PUBLISHERS
238 Seaboard Lane • Franklin, Tennessee 37067
www.providencehouse.com
800-321-5692

To Jim Adams

Jim Adams came to the *Cincinnati Post and Times Star* in the early 1960s. After many years as a religion reporter, Adams became an editor at the Post, eventually becoming the newspaper's chief editorial writer.

During his long tenure as religion reporter for the Post, he felt as comfortable questioning archbishops and rabbis as he did interviewing members of the Iron Horsemen motorcycle gang.

It was through his deep commitment as a Christian that he encouraged me and supported me in my ministry to the motorcycle gangs of the Midwest. He wrote a series of articles about the Iron Horsemen in 1970 that endeared him to them and developed a mutual relationship of trust and respect.

Jim Adams died on Wednesday, August 26, 2009.

FOREWORD

Our denominational numbers continue to decline because our constituency (middle-class whites) is declining and we need to learn how to be comfortable with the marginalized. That was Jesus' crowd! *Wear Your Collar* might be a needed encouragement in this endeavor. The story of how the Northside United Methodist Church learned to welcome gang members can be an exciting example of what the church of the twenty-first century must learn to do. Mainline denominations are dying. Revitalizations will come when we learn how to welcome ethnics and diverse socio-economic groups. *Wear Your Collar* is an exciting example of how this can happen, even in settings that are more complex than most congregations would face. The experience of Rev. Gene Skipworth was unique and we are enriched by the fact that he is sharing it with a wide audience. Reverend Skipworth, thank you.

—Bishop Emerson Colaw
retired Bishop of the United Methodist Church

ACKNOWLEDGMENTS

I would like to thank the following persons who contributed so much to the message of *Wear Your Collar*: Bill Garrett of Hanover, Pennsylvannia, who edited the manuscript; Ron Patterson of Nashville, Tennessee, who served as my agent; Bishop Emerson Colaw; the persons who provided testimonials on the back cover; Sue Straw, who digitized the photos; Terry Armor, photographer from the *Cincinnati Post and Times Star*; Bob Lyon, photographer from *Cincinnati Equirer*; Jim Adams, religion editor of the *Cincinnati Post and Times Star* (recently deceased) to whom the book is dedicated; the wonderful people of the Northside United Methodist Church; and the several bikers who allowed me, the church, and the message of Christ to embrace their lives and families.

INTRODUCTION

From 1969 to 1973, the church encountered new and different subcultures of our society. The women's liberation movement, the civil rights movement, and the anti-war movement were all confronting the church and society in general. Another subculture that emerged at that time was outlaw motorcycle gangs. *Wear Your Collar* is about how a minister and his congregation sought to reach out, get involved, and touch the lives of many of those gang members in the Cincinnati and Northern Kentucky area. The intent of the book is to provide a biblical imperative for the church to venture out into unique and different mission fields. The basic subject of the book is the uniqueness of that ministry to outlaw motorcycle gangs and what it entailed; how Reverend Skipworth became involved, how it affected the church he served, what effect it had on his family, the experiences he encountered, the lives and personalities of individual gang members, and the results of that ministry. Whether a person is involved in the church or not, *Wear Your Collar* will have an appeal to the reader due to the uncommon nature of the book. Newspaper reporters, novelists, and freelance writers have written about being with or riding with a gang such as described in Hunter Thompson's book *Hell's Angels*. But, riding with, ministering to, and becoming a closely trusted ally makes the story of wearing a collar with the Iron Horsemen and other outlaw bikers a different kind of read.

CHAPTER ONE

Little Jesus, a member of the Avengers outlaw motorcycle gang, stood in front of me with a switchblade in his right hand and a sick smile on his face. "I aim to find out what the preacher is made of," he bragged to his fellow Avengers.

Forty or so other motorcycle club members from the Satan's Angels, Satan's Sinners, Brothers In Arms, Iron Horsemen, Outlaws, and Devil's Disciples were there. Their mamas and old ladies (wives) began to form a circle around Little Jesus and me. They all wore their colors, which were well-worn blue denim sleeveless jackets with their club emblem on the back. The colors also had all kinds of badges, logos, symbols, and obscene wording.

I was pastor of the Northside United Methodist Church, an inner city church in Cincinnati. The Brothers In Arms was an outlaw motorcycle club whose member-ship centered around Northside. I was wearing their colors and served as their treasurer, because they said they couldn't trust anyone else. When I rode with them, they always said, "Wear your collar. We have a reputation to uphold."

I had seen Little Jesus on the streets around Clifton near the University of Cincinnati. Whenever I saw Little Jesus, he appeared to be high. He looked just like Captain Jack Sparrow in *Pirates of the Caribbean*.

We were in front of one of Cincinnati's chili parlors on Calhoun. Calhoun Street was where university students, hippies, druggies, the homeless, flower children, street people, and others of the counter-cultural movement hung out. They mingled among the bikers gathered around Little Jesus and me. I felt trapped.

Many outlaw bikers hung out on the street because that was where all the action took place. The center of all the street activity was around two acid rock dance hall dumps called the Black Dome and Reflections. They were places of complete chaos, constant trouble, loud noise, and pandemonium. It was common to see people smoking pot, strung out on dope and booze. Fights were frequent. And the bands played on.

A few weeks before the encounter with Little Jesus, several of us were in a sleazy cafe in Clifton near the Leather Shop late one night. It was next to Love's Coffee House where the street people gathered and the hippies would read their poetry and do their thing. Three Cobras and a half dozen other bikers were there, as well as some of the street people. We were talking about religion and the Bible and I had plenty of challenging and confrontational questions directed to me. One guy in particular raised some provoking questions. He looked like the typical street-freak. He had long shaggy hair, a long unkempt beard, sandals, dirty rumpled clothes, and used words and sentences characteristic of a dopehead. Often he used "Hey, man," "Whatta ya mean, man?" "Do ya dig it, man?" and quoted Timothy Leary, Bob Dylan, Allen Ginsberg, and other psychedelics. I imagined him to be a college dropout speed-freak that might have been a philosophy major, considering his occasional academic questions and vocabulary.

After the discussion, everyone left. The three Cobras and I were getting on our bikes parked along in front of the cafe. I asked one of them who the weird guy was asking all the questions. "He's a pusher here on the street, the biggest one. He has all the right contacts and is a real hustler. His name is Greenie because he has all the good green stuff." I thought how could a guy who brings so much harm and suffering to people sermonize and pontificate about life as he did in the discussion in the cafe.

As I was putting on my helmet and getting on my bike to leave, this pusher freak-head came out from the side of the building. Seeing him, I got off my bike and walked over to him with my best sermon face just for him. I didn't know what I was going to say, but I was going to say it with the best ecclesiastical trash-talk I could. My first words were, "I don't know anything about you but . . ." With that, he reached in his back pocket and pulled out a badge. He was a narcotics agent from the district attorney's office.

He said, "I've been watching you for about a month. I needed to find out if I could trust you. I need your help. Don't talk, just listen. My partner and I have been working the streets to put our case together and we are ready to make the bust. Make a contact for us to James Adams of the *Post and Times Star*, the writer who did the articles about you. We feel we can trust him. We want him here at a particular time

and place to cover this whole thing for us. Tell him to be ready for my call when it is going to come off." Then he left.

Greenie was standing behind the crowd when Little Jesus pulled his knife on me. It had been a few weeks since he had revealed his identity. Whenever we saw each other on the street, we kept our distance. We just nodded. We tried to give the impression that we didn't like each other, as if we were treading on each other's turf.

Greenie looked at me over the heads of the crowd. I knew that he was thinking: Now is the time to use what I taught you. I sure hope you didn't leave it at home. Several days before, he told me about his concern for my safety. He kept stressing, "These motorcycle gang members are unpredictable and volatile. They are always looking for a fight and you being a preacher doesn't make you immune." Little Jesus proved it.

I looked at Greenie with a nod, a confirmation that I was prepared. He had taught me well. He showed me how to make a weapon to use only in dangerous situations. It was a simple, perforated garden hose. Inside the hose, cotton was tightly compacted. The first thing I did before going out to be with any of the bikers was to saturate the cotton with mace or rubbing alcohol or most any liquid that would make a mess of someone's eyes when it splattered against them. I had a pocket sewn in the back of my colors to hold the hose. Whenever I was challenged or threatened, I would take out the hose and use it however I needed to protect myself.

Little Jesus stood in front of me. He had his knife in his right hand. He started moving to his right with that acid-laced smile and demonized eyes. I caught a quick glimpse of one of the hippies standing next to me on the left. I had seen her often on the street. She always looked bewildered and strung out and wore a small Viet Cong flag as a headband over her beautiful long black hair. In that short glimpse at her face, her eyes looked like a despondent nun about to witness Joan of Arc being burned at the stake.

No one in the crowd offered to step in and put a stop to this insanity. No one offered, "Stop this; don't you know he's a United Methodist minister?" None of the Brothers In Arms attempted to step in. I thought some of the mamas or old ladies would start screaming and that would put an end to this. Greenie gave me a look as if to say, "You are on your own. I can't step in. If I do, I will blow my cover." I needed someone to stop all this. All the bikers just stood there with beer bottles in their hands, looking like they were watching a card game.

I reached back and took the hose out of the pocket from the back of my colors. I hit Little Jesus before he made a move toward me. It surprised him. I hit him just once across the face and the mace and some of the cotton flew all over. He dropped the knife and covered his face with his hands. The adrenaline rush I felt was fear, but mostly anger. I hit him again with the hose and knocked him to the sidewalk. He didn't attempt to get up. Someone piled him into a car and left.

Five or six Avengers slowly walked to their bikes, staring me down all the way. I just stood there feeling their threatening and hostile looks. The president, a guy named Moose, said, "Preacher, it's gonna take more than a fuckin' hose next time."

Round, whose physical presence of six feet, two inches and three hundred pounds claimed the attention of everyone, was standing nearby. In addition to his size, he also possessed an amazing social and political power as president of the Iron Horsemen, the most feared outlaw club in the Midwest. Round said, loud enough for the Avengers and everyone else to hear, "Preacher, you don't need to worry about them or anybody from now on. We'll always have your ass covered."

Greenie smiled. I responded with a feeling of great relief. The bystanders looked at me with disbelief. I heard someone say, "Did you see what that preacher did?" Before anything else was said, I put the hose back in my jacket, got on my bike, gave Greenie a nod of thanks, and told Round, "I appreciated what you said," and went home.

Round's threat kept the Avengers, from Northern Kentucky, on the other side of the river and they eventually dropped from the biker scene. They were afraid to encounter any of the Horsemen who seemed always to be where bikers gathered. They knew that Little Jesus had put them on the bad side of the Horsemen.

Taking a beating by some motorcycle club members is a great way for a preacher to get their attention and eventually their trust, especially if the preacher keeps coming around. That's what happened with the Brothers In Arms. I took a beating from them, but kept showing up at the bar where they had their meetings, at some of their homes, the motorcycle shop where they met, and any place I saw them.

I was appointed as pastor, at the age of thirty-two, to the Northside United Methodist Church (NUMC) in January of 1969. It was one of eight inner-city churches in the Cincinnati District of the West Ohio Conference of the United Methodist Church. The NUMC was the typical mainstream inner-city church. At one time it had a large and active congregation. From 1962 to 1969, the membership had dropped from 356 to 216. The worship attendance had declined from 215 in 1961 to 78 in 1969. At Sunday morning worship it was very easy to find a place to sit because so many pews were empty. The congregation was older. I had far more funerals than weddings or baptisms.

The church was a magnificent stone building on Chase Avenue. It had one of the finest organs in the city. Students in the school of music from the University of Cincinnati came to practice on the organ. Scheduling the students and listening to them practice were two of my most enjoyable tasks.

When the neighborhood began to change in the early 60s, so did the congregation. Many of the members moved out when the first and second generation of white Appalachians began moving in along with a small percentage of blacks. Prior to 1960, the neighborhood was a middle-class German community just north of downtown Cincinnati. Two large Roman Catholic Churches of German origin—St. Boniface and St. Pius-X—were dominant in the community. The sidewalks in front of the brick row houses were always immaculately clean. As I walked the neighborhood, I would see a few of the remaining elderly German immigrants scrubbing the sidewalks in front of their homes.

During the late 60s and early 70s, I learned that my neighborhood was second only to Lower Price Hill's Eighth and State as the most violent and dangerous in the city. The Fifth District of the Cincinnati police department, which encompassed Northside, had the responsibility of keeping a lid on the turbulent and defiant community.

The church was surrounded by beautiful houses built at the turn of the century. Our parsonage was one of them. Each house was very close to the next with a small unattached garage in the back. This made it very easy for the postman to deliver the mail. Even in 1969, the mailman was a neighborhood character. He would often stop in for a cup of coffee and chat for a while. That was the only experience I had at Northside that might reflect the way things were years before I arrived.

There was litter and raw garbage from overturned garbage cans on the streets and sidewalks. Stray cats and dogs maneuvered around the drunks staggering along the sidewalk. Businesses that had closed left abandoned storefronts, many with their windows broken and doors torn off. Convenience stores put bars over their doors and windows. One of the characteristics of a blighted, depressed, rundown, and changing urban area is the number of used furniture stores that spring up. They took over buildings that were once fine clothing, drug, hardware, and grocery stores. The storefronts that were occupied were often storefront churches made up of the arriving white Appalachians with their own brand of mountain theology and worship. The names of their churches reflected their fundamentalist conservative Pentecostal biblical literalism theology: The Four Square Gospel Center of the Lord Jesus Christ, The High and Holy Tabernacle of God, The Temple of the Sanctified, and The Anointed Church of Christ.

I had a joint funeral with one of the storefront ministers at Miller Funeral Home. The oldest child of the family of the deceased attended the NUMC, while other members of the family attended the storefront. The family requested a particular Scripture to be read, but their minister couldn't read so he asked me to read it.

Their pastors were not trained or educated for ministry; they were simply "called of the Lord God, Almighty." Their worship started on Sunday morning and lasted into the afternoon. Sunday and Wednesday evenings they were in worship for more than two hours. Their worship did not include any liturgy or any organ music or hardback hymnals. Some of the churches used paperback hymnbooks, but most of the time they used songs with words which could be easily memorized and repeated over and over. Their instruments were guitars and tambourines. Their worship was very loud and animated. People gathered on the street in front to listen and watch the worship of the persons they called holy rollers.

Down the street from the parsonage was the most active business on Chase Avenue. It was a bar called Maria's. It was dirty, noisy, and open all night. I made several pastoral calls at the bar and I always wore my clerical collar. Wearing the clerical collar when I walked the streets and visited the bars gave me a naive feeling of protection and acceptance. I witnessed several fights in the bar. When I tried to break them up, the drunks just looked at me in amazement.

Maria's was a popular hangout for many of the outlaw biker clubs of the Cincinnati area. It served as the meeting place of the Brothers In Arms. The owner could not get a liquor license because he was a felon. Therefore, the bar was in his wife's name. One of the worst features of the bar was that it was near Chase Avenue Elementary. After school, kids walked past and couldn't pass up the chance to sneak a look at all that was going on. They saw drunks, fights, debauchery, and heard bawdy language. Often I saw two or three police cruisers with flashing lights parked out front.

All this made Northside the perfect place for an outlaw motorcycle club like the Brothers In Arms to take up residence. My first encounter with them was when I was a chaperone at a Northside Teen Association (NTA) dance held at the Northside Presbyterian Church (NPC). The NTA was organized by a group of concerned citizens, parents, business leaders, and church leaders.

The purpose of the NTA was to provide wholesome, supervised, and safe activities for the youth of the neighborhood. The most popular activity of the NTA was the dance held every other Friday night, alternating between the NUMC and the Northside Presbyterian Church. Bob Wilheit, a very active member of my congregation, was one of the organizers of the NTA. I looked to him for guidance on my first experience as a chaperone at an inner-city dance. He and his wife were among the few educated middle-class residents of Northside, and were always looking for ways to serve others.

Bob told me that the teenage population was very rough. School dropouts and truancy were serious problems and drug and alcohol abuse was common. Because of the number of teens involved in pre-marital sex, there were high rates of teen pregnancies and sexually transmitted diseases. Most of the kids lived in single-parent homes with little or no supervision.

Bob told me to expect to see the Brothers In Arms at the dance. I had never heard of the Brothers In Arms (BIA) until he mentioned them. They considered themselves to be the unofficial peacekeepers and chaperones at the dances. They were twenty to thirty years old, which made them too old officially, but they were always there. Bob explained that they took upon themselves the role of being in charge of anything that took place in Northside, and that included the NTA dances.

Only an hour had gone by when I began to feel some anxiety. After several checks on the men's restroom, I saw wine and beer bottles dumped in the trash cans and broken glass on the floor and in the urinals. There was the terrible smell of spilled booze. In spite of repeated warnings not to smoke, there was smoking in the restrooms as well as on the dance floor.

An older boy urinated in the corner of the dance floor. Two girls high on drugs ran screaming out the front door and down the outside steps into the traffic. One overweight kid named Bernie collapsed on the dance floor because he was high. We obviously didn't have enough chaperones for the one hundred seventy-five kids there. We could have used a nurse or two. But, we had only four women and three men. I kept wishing this dance was over. I told Bob, "I don't know about you, but I feel we are sitting on a keg of dynamite." I was feeling uneasy about everything.

I hadn't paid much attention to the Brothers In Arms. There were about a dozen of them sitting and standing behind the band at the end of the church gymnasium. They weren't doing anything to add to my anxiety. When I tried to engage them in conversation, I got only grunts. They never looked at me when I spoke to them. It

Filthy Phil

would have been helpful if they had volunteered or made some gesture to help settle down some of the nonsense going on.

When I thought things couldn't get any worse, things got bad, really bad. Several Harley Davidson motorcycles pulled up in front of the church with a loud thunderous roar. They belonged to about two dozen members of the Gladiators from Covington, Kentucky, a rival motorcycle club of the BIA. They had a score to settle with Filthy Phil, a leader of the BIA, who had roughed up a Gladiator a few days earlier. When they came onto the dance floor, they didn't have to search long. Filthy Phil knew who they wanted. Filthy was more than willing to oblige them. One of the Gladiators, who seemed to be their leader, began a fight with Filthy.

That was when I rose to the occasion. In 1968, I had competed in some amateur weightlifting competitions. I had more than four hundred pounds of weights in the basement of the parsonage and continued to work out. I was benchpressing three hundred fifteen pounds. I weighed 199 and had a 33-inch waist. It would be nothing, I thought, to step in and break up this fight. As I stepped in to stop the fight, other fights broke out between the two gangs. Undaunted, I waded in. Several of the teenage spectators screamed at me and cursed, "Leave them alone, you bastard, it's none of your damn business."

Then some of the bikers that were not in the fight yelled at me "Keep your ass out of this."

I yelled back, "Knock off this crap and get out of here." I was pushing and shoving and getting nowhere.

I was told by two of the Brothers In Arms, "Don't touch us, man. Nobody touches us."

Filthy Phil was knocked to the dance floor, unconscious. I was falling over chairs, legs, bodies, and musical instruments. Then the fight moved to the outside steps of the church. I went with it.

Bob tried to help break up some of the fighting. He was big into sensitivity training and now he really had a chance to practice his material. Before he had a chance to say anything, he got punched in the face and was lying unconscious on the church steps. He had a bloody face. His son Teddy, just thirteen, witnessed his dad getting decked and lying in a pool of blood.

I continued trying to break up the fights and defend myself. I yelled to the other chaperones, "Call the Fifth District." I learned early on that people did not refer to the police as "police" but as the "Fifth District." Where were they?

I didn't see the punch that landed on the side of my face. Then I got hit in the stomach. When I doubled over, a knee bloodied my nose. I went down and couldn't see a thing. Then I got kicked in the head and ribs. I realized then why those guys wore big boots. They made great weapons.

By this time Filthy Phil was back in the fight and was after the guy who started it all. It was a great relief when I heard the police sirens. At the sound of the sirens, the Gladiators straddled their bikes, stomped the kick-starters, and dodged traffic in a quick getaway. Just as quickly, the BIA disappeared on their Harleys. Two squad cars from the Fifth District pulled up. This must have been a common occurrence at NTA dances because the police seemed to have the attitude, "What happened this time?"

None of the kids at the dance said a word. They nonchalantly drifted down the street as if nothing had happened. Bob was up and around. Some of the women chaperones had taken him into the church office to tend to him. I had a big lump on the side of my head and was bleeding from my nose and left ear. My ribs hurt. Bob's wife came to pick up him and Teddy. The host minister, Tim Warren, began to close up. Those of us who were able began to clean up some of the mess. The police never took out notebooks to take notes. They just took a look at Bob and me and wanted to know if we wanted to file a complaint. I didn't know who to file it against. As he was helped into the car by his wife, Bob said, "I am not going to let Teddy come to anymore NTA dances."

I staggered the two blocks home with an ice-pack on the side of my face. I considered calling my bishop, Gerald Ensley, to tell him I did not want to serve an inner-city church after all. I did not like getting beaten up by neighborhood thugs. I had been at Northside less than a month and it was not what I thought it was going to be.

My concept of the inner-city church was one where I would walk the streets in an idyllic way like St. Francis walked through the woods and small villages and be the friendly cleric. I would find out who needed food, clothes, a friendly visit, and take care of all kinds of pastoral needs. The people would be appreciative and always be at the door of the church. They would respond to my charity by their Sunday morning attendance.

But the big, beautiful stone church building turned off these neighborhood residents. They were used to their small white, wood-framed church buildings in the hills of Appalachia. In Northside, their churches were the storefronts. They didn't know who St. Francis was and they didn't like some "collared" cleric coming down their street. If they wanted food, clothing, or pastoral care, they would ask for it from their own kind. My image of the inner-city church was that it would be a beacon of light and hope whose doors would always be open. I was very naive.

I found out the church doors always had to be locked. The neighborhood was not welcoming, even to a collared cleric. I found out, from my first NTA dance, that it was too tough and endowed with a propensity for lawlessness. It was no place for my kids. I thought of going back home to Illinois to teach again, or back to pastor a small rural parish.

The babysitter was shocked at the way I looked. Before she could ask what happened, Nancy, my six-year-old daughter, yelled down from her bedroom, "How was the dance, dad?" I didn't want to tell her that Bob got some teeth knocked loose and was roughed up. I was afraid I would frighten her if I told her that I also got the stuffings kicked out of me by two motorcycle clubs and one of them was here in Northside. I just told her it wasn't a good night and I doubted if we would ever have another dance. We had moved into the parsonage three weeks ago and I thought it might be best if we didn't finish unpacking our boxes.

While I took care of my cuts and bruises, the walls inside the house seemed to get taller and darker. The wallpaper had the illusion of cracking and peeling. I imagined the bathroom light flickering off and on like the neon Budweiser light in front of Maria's. As I soaked in the 1910 bathtub, all the darkness of despair closed in on me. Oh, for the quiet comfort of the rural parish.

Yale, my seven-year-old son, came in to use the bathroom. He took one look at me and had a shocked look on his face. "Dad, what happened to your eye?"

"A couple of drunks tried to get in the dance and I tried to get them away. Nothing serious happened. One of them just got in a lucky punch. I am just not a good boxer."

"Yeah, but you should have done better."

Soaking in the tub, I thought about the past three hours. Could the spirit of Christ penetrate this neighborhood? Could God use me to help those people see and experience Him? Could I make any difference to all those kids I saw tonight, especially the Brothers In Arms? Where would I start? Everything seemed so lost and despairing. No wonder members of the church moved out of this neighborhood. I would have moved, too.

There I was in a dark seventy-year-old house in a tough and unfamiliar neighborhood. Could I be an effective minister in what seemed, at that time, a hopeless appointment?

I prayed. I thought. I prayed more. I read Scripture. What was I going to do? Later that night, in the quiet darkness of the house, I made a decision. Since the Brothers In Arms existed in my own backyard, I needed to get involved.

My decision to reach out to the BIA, and hopefully, to other outlaw biker clubs in the Cincinnati area, came from my conviction that the church should be in ministry wherever there is a need. Too often the church spends its time ministering only to its own.

"The comfortable pew" describes the state of many churches. A great quote, attributed to a newspaperman more than a hundred years ago, Findlay Peter Dune, and one that uniquely fits the mission of the church, is, "Afflict the comfortable and comfort the afflicted."

CHAPTER TWO

The first test of this conviction for ministry was in my first appointment after ordination in June of 1966. I became the pastor of the Tiro Evangelical United Brethren Church, in the rural community of Tiro, Ohio. I often visited the local tavern and pool hall to try to become acquainted with some of the unchurched young adults of that community. I received a lot of flak from some of the members of the church. They said it was no place for a minister. I told them that Christ came to call sinners, not the righteous. They told me that I was not Christ. I tried to explain, "They will never see or experience Christ until we enter their world. They will never see or know that the doors of our church are open to them unless we reach out to them."

I only lasted two and a half years at my first appointment. I found out that not only did my church think I was wrong in going to the pool hall and bar, but they also didn't like it that I was also hanging out with Lutherans and Catholics. I am not sure which company they disliked most.

The church often points a judgmental and condescending finger at people who are different, who come from different racial, cultural, ethnic, and religious backgrounds, and different sexual orientations. Many churches have a sign that says "Everyone Welcome." That is not always the case. Individual bikers told me the church excluded them. Crazy Horse, a member of the Iron Horsemen, was very bitter toward the church. He described the church like the bumper sticker that said, "Church Makes God Look Ridiculous."

Filthy Phil loved to tell about the incident when he stopped at a traffic light and a church van from a Church of Christ pulled up next to him. The passenger rolled down his window and yelled, "You are going to burn in hell." Filthy said the light changed and the bumper sticker on the van said, "See you in church Sunday."

Intolerance was evident in the conversation I had recently with a church member who said that all Hispanics should learn English or go back to Mexico. Today the church voices its lack of tolerance for Muslims, immigrants, persons against the war, the role of women in the church, persons against the death penalty, the ordination of women, and homosexuals. In 1969, I found that many members of the NUMC had very little tolerance for greasers, or the white trash of Northside.

Our task as a church is to both tolerate and embrace diversity. We should let Christ's love rid us of fear, enabling us to abound in grace in our care for persons in need. We should let Christ's love rid us of our personal prejudices and let them be touched and transformed by the love of God. United Methodist Bishop C. Joseph Sprague and fellow inner-city colleague of the late 60s, says in his book *Affirmations of a Dissenter* that there are people in the church:

> *who are vexed in the deepest recesses of their souls with the attempted takeover of the church by closed minds and fearful hearts, which seek security in rigid literalism, narrow parochialism, and hurtful exclusivism.*

Jesus tells us five times why He came. In Mark 2:17, in *The Living Bible,* he said, "I haven't come to tell good people to repent, but the bad ones." The Bad Ones was one of over twenty outlaw motorcycle clubs in the Cincinnati area whose names reflected where they felt they were in relation to the rest of society and the love of God: Devil's Disciples, Satan's Sinners, Satan's Angels, Nobody's Children, Outlaws, Midnight Drifters, Renegades, Nomads, Fugueros (Spanish for fugitive), Lost Souls, Lost Children, Animals, Gladiators, Henchmen, Coffin Cheaters.

After the fight at the Northside Teen Association dance, Bob made it to church the next Sunday after we were beaten. There were lots of questions raised when people saw our swollen lips and closed and puffy eyes. Many people already knew what had happened. Some of the church members who had moved away, but came back to worship each Sunday, told us, "That's why I voted against those dances being held in our church. Now that you have been beat up maybe you will stop all this. We don't want to see our building torn up when we walk in here on Sunday morning. Let alone, our minister."

I had a meeting with our District Superintendent Dr. Howard Brown. He had heard about the dance and what had taken place. I told him I wanted to continue the neighborhood ministry started by previous ministers, and that I also wanted to minister to the Brothers In Arms and eventually the twenty-plus outlaw motorcycle clubs in Cincinnati. He said, "If you are willing to take the risk, I will do everything I can to support you." It was very encouraging when he told me he would talk to Bishop Ensley to enlist his support.

I was going to have a problem with the long-time church members. They considered the NUMC *their* church. Their parents belonged there, they were baptized there, their kids were baptized there, their kids were married there, and this was *their* church. They moved out of Northside to get away from the people moving in. When they came back on Sundays to worship, they didn't want *those* people in *their* church. Attempting to continue to minister to the neighborhood as my predecessors had done, and to become involved with the BIA, was going to be a difficult task.

The members of my church knew the bikers existed in Northside. They had seen the Brothers In Arms in the neighborhood. They had read about the fights, shootings, and lawlessness of the BIA. After I talked to Dr. Brown, I talked to the administrative board of the church. I stressed how the Brothers In Arms should be a part of our mission. When I presented the concept of extending our neighborhood ministry to include the Brothers In Arms, and eventually other motorcycle clubs, there were several strong dissenting opinions. Including the bikers in our outreach only served to intensify the friction between pulpit and pew.

I felt a great deal of tension and inner turmoil in what I was asking my congregation to do. I was afraid I was asking too much of those church members who, just like me, had never faced such a challenge. I thought I could be pushing the envelope too far in introducing this new mission for the church. I faced the risk of tearing the church apart for the sake of trying to reach out to a gang of wild, stoned, womanizing bikers who have never shown any interest in the church, let alone an interest in letting Christ come into their lives.

Many of them asked, "What will people think if our minister is involved with this sort? Have you seen them? They look horrible. What will people think when those troublemakers park their motorcycles in front of our church or parsonage? We don't want our minister to be seen associating with that bunch."

Other members of the board expressed similar statements: "You must be nuts for messing around with those idiots. You are going to get yourself in trouble. Don't you care about the church? Don't you care about your family? Don't you care about your reputation? You will be wasting your time with those filthy, no-good gangs. They should be locked up and never seen again."

I had been at the NUMC for only three weeks, but I began to understand why this inner-city church was still white, middle-class, and uninvolved in the community. We never had any neighborhood people attend worship, let alone, join. We had very few children and none from the neighborhood. The church was open only on Sundays. I had mentioned to the education committee of the church when I first arrived about having a weekday after-school program for the elementary school children. They told me, "We don't want our carpeting to be messed up with all those kids in here."

I began to get discouraged at the board meeting when I heard only negative comments about the church getting involved. But soon others began to speak up in support. Barb Lambing, Jewel Smith, and others began to affirm the possibilities of this new mission for our church. Mr. Waldkamp, who lived down the street from the church and ran a film rental business, said, "Reverend Skipworth, I'll be glad to do whatever I can to allow you more time to work with these young men. We certainly ought to do something to try to reach them."

After he broke the ice, more persons began to speak in support of reaching out to the BIA and others in our community who needed the message of Christ's love. Many were skeptical, but decided to go along with it to see how "Skipworth's idea" was going to pan out.

I felt confident this was the mission to which God was calling me and the church. In Matthew 9:11, Jesus' disciples were asked by the religious leaders, "What kind of example is this from your Teacher, acting cozy with crooks and riffraff?" (THE MESSAGE). It was up to us to extend the shepherding care of Christ to the riffraff.

I had some ideas about riffraff. I grew up in St. Elmo, Illinois, a small town in the central part of the state. Whenever I went downtown with my mom, we crossed the street before we got near the pool hall. She said the pool hall was "full of riffraff." That was the first time I had ever heard about riffraff.

Now I was faced with reaching out to outlaw motorcycle clubs?

Colin Williams, dean of the Yale Divinity School, said "The ministry of the church must exist to make Christ available, to exist for others."

I had no skills for such an undertaking. I took courses in seminary on missions and evangelism, but the courses centered on the parochial and had a narrow outlook. The mission emphasis was foreign missions, not with the Hell's Angels.

I knew nothing about reaching out to outlaw motorcycle clubs. Where would I start? What would I say to them? How would I approach them? The only thing I

had going for me (and I wasn't sure that was positive) was the experience of being beaten by some Gladiators and Brothers in Arms.

When it came to ministering to motorcycle gangs, I was afraid. I was afraid physically. I didn't want to get beaten again. I was strong and in shape, but there were risks that had to be taken. I was afraid mentally. I didn't know if I could make the right split-second decisions that would be "smart." I didn't know if I could give the right answers to difficult questions an aggressive biker might throw at me. I was afraid spiritually. Such a venture really was going to test my faith. I needed to know how to represent Christ in a whole new and different environment. I was afraid emotionally. Could I stand the pressure? Could I handle the risk of alienating my congregation and creating possible divisiveness there? How was this going to impact my family?

Before I even thought about getting involved with the BIA or any other outlaw biker club, the NUMC wasn't considering outlaw bikers as a mission. The district superintendent didn't have expectations of my ministering to bikers. The bishop did not appoint me to Northside to work with bikers. I had no colleagues, at this point, encouraging me. There was no other church involved in such a mission that I could call on for help. There was no model to go by.

The church I was serving was right in the middle of a motorcycle club's territory. I was the church's minister who had been beaten by that biker club.

I faced a very difficult decision. Do I get involved or not? I wanted to make the right decision and one that reflected what God wanted me to do.

I needed to have confirmation from God. That confirmation also depended on the willingness of my church to accept this challenge. The district superintendent had already voiced support. The bishop had sensed the importance of this ministry. It would be a wonderful affirmation to have the encouragement of my denomination as well.

I was a preacher, and the apostle Paul was very specific, and he could have had people like the Brothers In Arms in mind, when he said, "How will they hear without a preacher?" I seemed to be the right preacher at the right time and in the right place. Who else qualified like I did? I had an interest in motorcycles. I raced motorcycles. I was a bodybuilder/weightlifter and those guys judged a person from the neck down.

But, I had no spiritual gifts for this calling. I had to accept this new venture through faith that I was the right man for this mission.

I liked challenges and getting involved with outlaw biker clubs was certainly going to be a challenge. I wasn't going to do this on my own. "The field is ripe for harvest" and I was going to have help from the Master. I was going to need His help if I was going to bring His love to the riffraff, those who were unaccepted by society and most churches. I wanted them to know that God cared for them and that the Church cared for them.

I needed to enable my church to see we were in this mission together.

Dr. Donald W. Haynes, special contributor to the *United Methodist Reporter*, said, "Churches daring to re-vision will anchor themselves in the future, not the past. Try re-visioning 'thy kingdom come, thy will be done in our church as it is in heaven.'"

I wished I could have told the administrative board that there was a brochure published by Abingdon Press of the United Methodist Church on "How to Reach Outlaw Motorcycle Gangs" that we could use as our guide in our ministry. It would have been useful if there had been another church that had accomplished a similar ministry from which we could learn.

None of my seminary files or textbooks included anything on ministry to outlaw motorcycle clubs. There was no book entitled *Reaching Out to Motorcycle Clubs for Dummies*. Churches have ventured out to reach the outcasts of society in many ways, but for me and the Northside United Methodist Church, it was going to be a whole new experience.

Bob Wilheit joined other board members who spoke in favor of accepting this challenge of reaching out to the BIA. He suggested we go ahead with plans for the next dance, which was scheduled at our church. He said we needed to make extra preparations this time and do everything we could to prevent any trouble.

He said the first thing to do was enlist plenty of chaperones. "Big ones," he said. Clarence Pate, the huge Northside Baptist minister who played football in college, was invited to be one. I went to the University of Cincinnati physical education department and explained to one of the deans why I wanted four or five big male physical education students. He helped me recruit four. One of them was a manager for the football team and after I talked to him about what I wanted, he recruited three of the football players. I called the Fifth District police department to make sure they patrolled the block around the church. I told the officer I talked to, "If you see a motorcycle come near the church, send a squad car and pull up immediately, we don't want any trouble this time." Three church members purchased more weights and another weightlifting bench to be placed in the basement of the parsonage. If the BIA showed up, we hoped we could get some of them to go over to the parsonage to lift weights.

One of the couples of the church suggested we have hosts to represent the church, in addition to the chaperones. The hosts would serve as greeters from the NUMC. Dale and Mary Hopper made the suggestion and volunteered. They had never met a BIA and considered this an opportunity to get involved firsthand.

When it came time for the dance, my fears were confirmed; the BIA were the first ones there. Their Harleys were parked on Delaney Street at the main entrance of the church. So much for the Fifth District surveillance.

More than a dozen of them were waiting on the front steps of the church. Chains and leather straps hung from their colors, they wore black leather gloves, blackjacks dangled from their belt loops, they wore motorcycle chains for belts around their greasy, dirty jeans (sprocket chains were used for weapons), and they had their Nazi helmets in hand. They wore the big, black cycle boots that I knew so well.

My first words to the president, Butch, were, "How you doing?" He said nothing. "No one else here yet?" No response. "Your club colors look pretty good. Can I see them?"

I was really surprised when he looked me in the eye and said, "Yeah, man."

I found out later that their colors were their basis for identity and meaning. They had a great deal of pride in their colors and were loyal to them. When I took an interest, they tuned in.

"Who designed these for you?"

Filthy Phil responded quickly, and with a great deal of pride, "I did."

Surprised at being acknowledged, and not knowing what to say next, I blurted out, "I am thinking of buying a motorcycle, could you help me? I don't know much about them. I don't know about cost or where the best place is to get one. Could you give me some advice on what to do?"

Butch said, "Yeah, we'll see you Tuesday night."

Just as Butch said that, Roach and Cherokee, two other BIA, started to bring their bottles of wine into the church. I didn't give them a big hassle; I just told them to take the bottles across the street and empty them and put them in a trash can.

Next, the Gladiators showed up; my biggest nightmare. Where on earth were the cops? Surely they heard these guys come up Hamilton Avenue. They pulled their

19

bikes across the street from the bikes of the BIA. I told them before they got off their bikes they weren't welcome. Then I walked away with my back to them. Out of the corner of my eye, I saw one of them get off his bike, cross the street and begin walking behind me. I heard him, a guy named Cowboy, say that he was going to bust a beer bottle over my head. I just kept on walking like I didn't hear him. I was scared to death. There was no way to predict what these guys would do. I was hoping he was not the kind of thug who would hit me when my back was turned to him. It was like the Wild West; who would shoot a guy in the back? I heard one of his brothers say, "Let him go, Cowboy."

Just then, two of the University of Cincinnati male students I had recruited came out the church door where the Gladiators were parked and asked, "Any trouble out here?" Cowboy threw the bottle against the stone wall of the church and it shattered into a million pieces. Then he got on his bike and they all left. The thunder of their bike engines had an angry sounding blast to them. Surely such noise got the attention of the Fifth District as the Gladiators rumbled down Chase Avenue. But, the Fifth District would be about an hour too late.

Butch said they would see me on Tuesday night. It seemed so easy! They didn't know me except that I was the preacher they beat up at the last dance. My feelings of optimism increased as some of the BIA responded to Dale and Mary's invitation to go over to the basement to lift weights. Others stayed at the dance to make sure no problems occurred. It was as if they had a newfound sense of keeping peace on the church property, just like being pit bulls, protecting me, my kids, and the church.

I was enthused and expectant on the Tuesday night following the dance. I was thinking how fantastic it was that I had made such an inroad so early with the BIA. But as the night went on, that feeling of optimism went down the drain. They didn't show up. They had no intentions of coming over and they had no intentions of letting me get to know them.

Ten-thirty came and I was ready to chalk it up as a lost cause. My hopes kept fading until I heard a knock on the door at eleven o'clock. A young man at the door wanted to know if this was where the Brothers In Arms was meeting. I told him they were supposed to come over but they weren't going to have a meeting.

Soon after he left, sixteen Harley's woke up the neighborhood as they pulled into my driveway. They didn't knock; they just came into the house. Butch said they were going to have their meeting and that I should sit off to the side. My kids were

Butch, president of Brothers in Arms, and Filthy Phil

upstairs in bed and I did just as he said. They began to take off their leather jackets which they wore under their colors. I saw knives in small holsters attached to their boots and some had revolvers stuck in their cycle chain belts. That was when I thought, "What have I gotten myself into?"

The meeting started and the creed was repeated in unison, "I pledge I will not disgrace the name of this club. I also pledge to help any brother that is in any need. For the motto of the club is one percent always. 'All for one and one for all.'" On that night they were going to vote on two prospective members who had served as pledges for three months. One was voted in and the other was voted on and failed and was told to leave.

Then Butch said, "Preacher, we voted on you already to be our treasurer. Do you have a basement?" I told him I did.

He asked, "Can we meet here in your basement next week? Maria's don't work too good. Cops show up too often."

I told him yes and everyone left except him and his mama and a couple of other Brothers. We talked a little about motorcycles and the "club," as they called themselves. As they were preparing to leave, I asked Butch, "Why did you ask me to be your treasurer?"

He said, "We didn't ask you, we told you. You're going to be our treasurer because we can't trust anybody else. Besides, the cops are tryin' to wipe us out by arresting us for all kinds of shit, like lookin' at old ladies and makin' noise. They are always watching us. The narcs are on our backs and so is this whole fuckin' neighborhood. The whole thing stinks like shit. You're the only citizen that hasn't bitched at us. You're the only preacher we know.

"We also liked the way you handled Roach and Cherokee when they started to bring those wine bottles in the church. You didn't bitch at them or nothin'. And when the Gladiator showed up you let everybody know you were the main man."

My worries about building a relationship with the Brothers In Arms were overcome. Early the next morning, Butch came to the house to show off his motorcycle. This was my first encounter with what was most important to motorcycle clubs. The colors were important, but the bike was a reflection of who they were: loud, strong, and very visible. It was their prize possession.

Riding with the BIA for a couple of months helped me meet other outlaw bikers in the Cincinnati area. The clubs and the people who hung around them came to know me as "the preacher," the "biker chaplain," or the "outlaw preacher."

Eventually a couple of the BIA showed up for worship. They were curious to find out whether I really was a minister. Filthy Phil and Sarge were the first two BIA to show up. Sarge came a second time and brought his girlfriend to show her that "he wears a black robe and everything."

As this mission of the NUMC to the BIA became more acceptable and active, other neighborhood ministries were developed by the church. We began a food and clothing pantry. I found out that churches could provide a breakfast program with which the Department of Agriculture helped. I went to the Federal Building downtown and visited a lady who was the resource person. Through her help we were able to provide a breakfast for the neighborhood children every Wednesday.

We also began an after-school program which provided recreation, snacks, arts and crafts, and help for the older girls in caring for their younger brothers and sisters. The after-school program also offered tutoring.

For help in the after-school program, I enlisted several high school students and their youth leaders from United Methodist Churches in Mt. Healthy, North College Hill, and Forest Park. One of those young men was a star baseball player for Mt. Healthy High School and I recruited him to play baseball for the University of Illinois. These young people and their adult leaders also helped establish a day camp opportunity for the children of Northside. There were several who helped the NUMC people make these programs a very important ministry to the Northside neighborhood.

My relationship to the Brothers In Arms became more enhanced as our ministry to Northside grew. They saw the church caring for others, including them. They stopped by the house more often. They offered to do things around the house. They would babysit for me when I had a quick call to make. One day two of the trustees of the church were doing some work in the kitchen and a couple of guys who were hanging out at the parsonage offered to help.

I had to go to United Seminary in Dayton to pick up a book and visit a professor from whom I was taking a graduate course. As I was getting ready to leave, five members of the BIA came by the house. They asked where I was going. When I told them, they asked if they could go along since they weren't doing anything. (They hardly ever had anything to do.)

I had a suit and tie on and they asked me to change and wear the BIA colors since they were wearing theirs. They said, "We should tork that preacher factory out of shape." I wasn't too sure about this whole idea but it did sound kind of interesting. So, I put on my colors, boots, and Levis and we took off in my car. It was February and too cold to ride up on our bikes.

When we got to the seminary, we parked in front of one of the dorms. The first place they wanted to visit was the dorm because they said, "We want to see some nuns."

Another said, "I really got a feelin' those wenches are really good-looking under that garb."

I had no idea what kind of seminary they thought they had come to.

When we got to the dorm, we went downstairs to the large basement where some of the students' children have their bicycles. A student happened to be down there and the guys started their image-role-play game with him. "Hey, man, we are looking for a place to work on our bikes. This basement looks real nice. It is clean, warm, and I bet some nice wenches come around once in a while. Do you think you can arrange for us to get our bikes down here to work on?"

I began to wonder if it was a good idea for these guys to come to the seminary with me.

The student fell right into their game. "Well, I don't know. You will have to talk to the dean."

"Where's da dean at?" Filthy Phil was really getting the guy going. "Do you know him? Is he a bad dude, or is he fine and cherry? Does he know cool? What's his mind?"

"Yes, he is a pretty nice man. You will find him in the administration building."

The student started to walk off in a rush because he hadn't had a course in seminary on how to converse with outlaw bikers. Filthy stopped him in his tracks with, "Hey, baby, we ain't stopped spreadin' it around with you. You are supposed to be a kind host. You don't even know who I am. What's my number, man?"

The student forced a smile and said, "What else can I do for you?"

Sarge saw all the fun Filthy was having and wanted some, too. "Where's the dean's place again? Show us."

I knew Dean Newell Wert very well and did not want to embarrass myself or get myself in any trouble. I was having second thoughts about the guys coming with me.

After pointing us in the right direction, we started walking toward the administration building. As we walked, the guys were asking me where I lived when I was in seminary, if I knew the student we had just talked to, where all the girls were, if seminary was hard, did I like it, and several other questions. By this time word had gotten around that some Hell's Angels had just arrived and were taking over the seminary. As we were on our way to the administration building, a good friend of mine who was on the staff of the seminary came out of the administration building to check on all the commotion. He came right toward us. The guys asked me if I knew him. I said, "Yes, he's a good friend of mine."

Cherokee asked, "Is he an alright guy or will he get you in trouble for us coming here?"

I told them that he was a fun guy and was always ready for a practical joke. Butch said, "OK, preacher, you get behind Cherokee and Tony and we will give him some pearls."

"Hi, fellows," my friend said to the five Brothers. "Can I help you?"

"Yeah, man, where is the preacher factory?"

"You're at it. What can I do for you?"

Sarge said, "We want to join."

At that time, my friend saw me behind the others and couldn't believe it. "Skipworth, what are you doing? What's going on?" And then he started laughing.

He was one of several students and faculty who knew of my ministry to the bikers in the Cincinnati area. As he began laughing, I could see the wheels turning in his head. He was thinking of some devilment to get into.

After the introductions were over, Filthy told him about our conversations with the student in the basement of the dorm. My friend made a suggestion. "Listen, soon a homiletics class is going to start. Skip, you know where the class is. You guys go in there and take seats in the back row and see what happens."

The Brothers went bananas. They were about to attend their first homiletics class.

The homiletics professor, Dr. Edwin Burtner, was always ready to show a lighter side of his academic role. When he saw me come in accompanied by the Brothers In Arms, and my friend outside the door grinning, he nodded a welcome to us all as we settled in our places in the back of the room.

After a student finished preaching his sermon assignment for the class and sat down, Dino walked up to the podium, unannounced, and did an impromptu sermon. It was short but filled with energy and "conviction." The Brothers were strong in the "Amen" section. Filthy and Sarge took a collection and got twenty-three cents.

Months after that experience, the Brothers In Arms told several biker clubs what my friend at the seminary and I had done with them. From that time on I began to be considered less and less of a jag to the BIA. Other outlaw clubs also began to recognize me as the "preacher" in a positive way.

As time went on and my reputation began to grow, other bikers would show up for worship. Some of the church members were very uncomfortable seeing outlaw bikers come into the sanctuary with obscene badges and four-letter words embroidered on their colors sitting next to them in worship. Some of the bikers came from all-night booze parties, some were strung out on dope, and some had spent Saturday night in jail. The church members didn't like to see them so unprepared for worship—no suits, no ties, long hair, smelly dirty clothes.

We had some church members who were from Germany. Seeing a biker come in with his Nazi helmet in his hand and swastika emblem on his colors tested their tolerance. But two of the older and long-time members who were from Germany were always warm and gracious in their welcome to those who came. When some of the skeptics saw the bikers straggle in occasionally to attend worship, their attitudes began to change. Sometimes the little things the bikers did for some of the church members helped change attitudes.

For instance, one of the ladies who did not endorse the ministry to the "motorcycle hoods," as her husband called them, was at a meeting at the church. When the meeting was over she went to her car and found that she had locked her keys in her car. She came back in the church, upset and angry at herself. I told her to wait a minute. I went over to the house and Grease was there watching television with a couple of other Nomads. I brought him back to the church and explained to him the lady's problem. He said, "That's easy. It won't take but just a minute." Doing "his thing," with some of the "tools" and several keys he had attached to a long chain on his jeans, he opened the car door for her. She thanked him and asked him his name. "I am Grease."

She told him, "I hope to see you again."

Filthy Phil displayed his magic one time for the president of the United Methodist Women. She came to the parsonage to tell me that she had forgotten her church key and wanted to know if she could use mine. Filthy, who was visiting, said he would take care of it. He didn't take my key; he just had the lady follow him to the church. Somehow, with some of the "tools" he had on him, he opened the church door.

During one of my speaking engagements, an artist who happened to be present sketched a picture of what I described during a worship service. My description of what took place involved Jake, a Coffin Cheater. We had a semi-circle altar rail in the chancel where we would gather to receive the elements for Holy Communion. One Sunday, Jake came to communion and stood at the rail to receive the elements. He had on the back of his colors, "Fuck the World." He knelt at the altar rail to receive the elements with the other communicants and received the tokens of Christ's body and cup for forgiveness and at-one-ness with God.

He had no intentions of putting on such a gross display of disrespect, or of offending anyone, or embarrassing me or anyone in the pews. His colors were such an intrinsic part of him that he was totally negligent of the offensive words with his back facing the congregation.

When worship was over, one of the young men of the church, Alan North, was ushering and pointed out to him what he had done. Jake felt very sorry, embarrassed, and promised he would never bother us again. Then Alan simply said, "No, Jake, we are glad to see you. Next time, it might be best if you left your colors on the coat rack before you enter the sanctuary."

Jake came back to worship once in a while, but he never wore his colors. He and Alan and Alan's family developed a friendship that Jake never had anywhere else outside his brothers in the Coffin Cheaters.

During the Lenten Bible study series in 1969, some of the BIA began to attend. As the study continued, some of them became good contributors to the discussions

that took place. They raised challenging questions not only to me but also to members of the church. Some of the mamas and old ladies of the bikers started showing up. When members of other clubs, or a girl, or a street thug were looking for a particular BIA, they would come to the room where we were meeting in the church and tell them they were wanted.

Once, Dino had a kid from the neighborhood come to the room and call him out. "Hey, Dino, we got a thing outside you better check into." When he left and returned from his "business," he sat down and got back into the discussion. Every Wednesday night during Lent, all the youth of Northside and other biker clubs knew where the BIA could be located.

Grease contemplates his good deed

One night during the study sessions, Tony asked the members of the church a challenging question. Faye Flynt from the district office was there. I told her about the BIA attending the study and she wanted to come and experience it for herself. The biker stood up and said, "Let's stop everything for a minute, I got a question to ask. This has nothing to do with what we are talking about. I want to change the subject. I got something on my mind and I want to run it down to everybody here. What do you people REALLY think about us and about us being here?" He sat down. The room was very quiet. I waited to hear what the response of the people would be.

Mrs. Flynt had a big smile on her face as if to say, "OK, folks, what ARE you going to say?" That was one of her characteristics, a great smile. She was near retirement age but the most alert, energetic, creative, enthusiastic, and one of the most able Christian leaders I had ever met. She always had fresh ideas, a ready wit, and was never afraid to accept or listen to new ideas for the church's work. She was one of the most enthusiastic and interested supporters of my ministry to motorcycle gangs. She had written the following article ("Preacher on a Motorcycle") about me in the district newsletter just days before. This is what it read:

Would you believe it? Zooming down the expressway came a young man on a motor-cycle: black jacket with the gang insignia on his back, helmet, goggles, and a clerical collar around his neck. That's pastor Skipworth, otherwise known as "Skip."

Skip infiltrated a gang of young men through being there when a fight broke out. Here were eighteen young men, all with criminal records, some out on bail, but they have come to trust Pastor Skip.

The parsonage basement is a gang "hangout" where they lift weights and talk for endless hours with their friend. Here in Skip's home they come in contact with a loving man and his family. A number have attended the Lenten suppers and participated in the discussions with the church members. Some have "tried out" morning worship, and one asked to be baptized.

And now? Some are employed, some in prison, some in jail, but Skip, well, he's their great friend.

Mrs. Flynt and I were waiting for a comment to break the silence. One of the older ladies of the church said, "Well, we are glad to see you coming here. At first I was very skeptical and wasn't too sure that I wanted you here. But now that I have gotten to know you, I am glad you are here and hope you will keep coming."

As challenging as the question was from the biker, an equally challenging question was raised by one of the church members. "If Rev. Skipworth was not here anymore, would you be here? Are you here because of him or do you really want to come to church?"

Bones said, "Sure we're here because of the preacher but we been diggin' what's been goin' on here. Besides, the food is cherry."

Jewel Smith spoke up next. Jewel was one of the ladies of the church who helped me begin the breakfast program and after-school program for the elementary school children of the neighborhood. She began a food and clothing pantry in our church building that became known as the Northside Food Pantry, later named the Jewel Smith Pantry, on Hamilton Avenue. She was also on the district steering committee that helped me in my ministry to the motorcycle clubs.

She said to the lady who raised the issue, "If Rev. Skipworth leaves and these young men and their friends stop coming, it won't be Rev. Skipworth's fault. It will be ours. We have the responsibility to continue the relationship he has built with these young men. That is the way it is with anyone who comes to the church from the neighbor-hood. It's our responsibility to provide an atmosphere of welcome."

On the last night of the study, the BIA brought a large sheet cake. It was elaborately decorated and iced with all kinds of statements like, "We dig you" and "God is cool." The cake was signed, "The Brothers In Arms." They made a formal presentation of the cake and said, "We been comin' here all these Wednesday nights and instead of freeloading again, we wanted to contribute something." Filthy Phil had baked and decorated the cake.

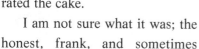
Cobras arrive for Lenten Study

I am not sure what it was; the honest, frank, and sometimes confrontational conversation (which was characteristic of outlaw bikers), the novelty of wearing colors among respectful and gracious people, associating with church folk who embraced them, or the good food, but the BIA, as well as a few Cobras, kept coming back to the Lenten study.

The presence of outlaw bikers in worship and other functions of the church pushed the tolerance and patience of some church members to the limit. When they found that the district superintendent and the bishop were supportive of me in this ministry, several of them transferred to churches where they would not have to deal with these kind of people. A few other members of the church continued to be involved, hoping I would go away and the bikers with me.

Several weeks later, I was with the Iron Horsemen and mentioned the discontent that some of the church members had with me. Round told me, "You better learn and learn fast, preacher, that if you want to make it there, you're going to have to start sucking some butts. You keep hanging around us and having us over to your house, the church people are always going to get in your face. Hell, preacher, you got toys upstairs."

CHAPTER THREE

Over the next several months, I had ridden with the Brothers In Arms, Devil's Disciples, Cobras, Henchmen, and others. I wanted to reach out to the top and undisputed leaders of the outlaw element of the bikers in the Cincinnati area, the Iron Horsemen. I wanted my ministry to the bikers to reach the very core, the heart of the outlaw subculture rather than just the bikers on the fringe.

The Iron Horsemen were the envy of every outlaw biker club in the Midwest. Many who had aspirations to be outlaw bikers wanted to be an Iron Horseman. They wanted to be a Horseman because the Horseman got more respect than all the other bikers in the Midwest. They wanted to wear the Horseman colors because everyone knew about the Horseman. Being a Horseman meant you were always where the action was. Being a Horseman, they thought, was to be a winner. Being a Horseman meant you belonged to a brotherhood which was stronger and tighter than any other.

Crazy Horse, a Horseman who had a great vocabulary, was very articulate, and seemed to be one of the more intelligent ones, said in regard to their brotherhood: "We have a stronger koinonia than any church." Crazy Horse looked like he had been a middle linebacker in college. I often wondered if he was a college dropout because he just didn't seem to fit the image of an Iron Horseman. Newspaper reporter from the *Cincinnati Enquirer* David Wells described him as "An immense man with busy hair, beard and a single dangling earring. Crazy Horse verbalizes very well and in that sense he is different from the stereotypes of bikers." Crazy Horse is still a large part of his personality. And, nobody messed with him.

Television and newspaper coverage belonged to the Iron Horsemen. Because of their constant publicity, they were well known not only to the public, but also with

Biking Is In His Blood

Crazy Horse

editors, reporters, and photographers of the local newspapers and television stations. They had the éclat, which enabled them to call a television station to ask for and get coverage when they wanted to make an announcement about one of their activities. Their extremist looks, behavior, reputation, and statements brought out the reporters and cameras. They became well known for their criminal activity, gang wars, and run-ins with the police. Al Shottlecotte, a local television news commentator, disliked the Iron Horsemen so much he accused them of causing rumbles, hassles, fights, and crimes when he knew they weren't responsible. They often complained that the publicity they received was always unfavorable to them.

One such incident occurred when four Bridgetown teenagers, involved in a two-car accident near the Iron Horsemen clubhouse in Delhi Township, told police the Iron Horsemen threw beer bottles at them and caused the accident. One sixteen-year-old boy involved in the accident filed assault and battery charges against one of the Horsemen. Because the Horsemen were involved, the Hamilton County and Delhi Township police converged on the scene in droves.

The newspaper reported, "The Horsemen say police frisked them at gunpoint, tossed furniture around the clubhouse and then took all of them to the Hamilton County Communications Center to be fingerprinted. One of the Horsemen was charged. All the others were released."

Rankled by what he considered a bad bust and the publicity that it had attracted, Round, the president of the Iron Horsemen, contacted a writer of one of the newspapers. Round wanted to tell their side of the story. The reporter wrote the following:

He arranged for me to meet with him and several other Horsemen at his apartment on Amity Road. Round was working on a motorcycle in his backyard when I got there. His blond wife and little boy were in the house watching television. Another Horseman, Doug, in trouble with police on a bail-jumping charge, was staying with them. Round came in the house. It was easy to guess how he got his name. He weighs more than 300 lbs. Round is an articulate leader with a loud, infectious laugh. He obviously has the respect of his troops.

Round explained to the reporter what had happened by starting with, "Let me run it down to you." He closed his comments by saying, "That story on the bust was a jag, man, a stone jag." There were many other calls to the media to "set things straight."

Horsemen ready to ride

The bad publicity about the Horsemen created other problems for them. One was when the Horsemen were run out of their meeting house which they had been renting. The community where the meeting house was located put a lot of pressure on the landlord to get the Iron Horsemen out of the house and out of the neighborhood. Round asked me to go with him to a meeting with their landlord and some of the neighbors. Round said, "Wear you collar."

We met at the landlord's house. We talked. Round told him and a few of the neighbors, "We have this high-powered lawyer who is a friend of our preacher. If we have to, we will take you to court."

One of the neighbors said, "We already know of some of the trouble you have had with the law. No citizen will allow you to bring that to their neighborhood. Just on a practical note, can you guarantee you will not break our noise ordinance?"

The Horsemen lost this one, too. They didn't have many people in their corner.

There were many reasons why the Horsemen were the elite of outlaw bikers in Southern Ohio, Indiana, and Northern Kentucky. They had more weapons, longer jail and prison records per man, more members on parole and probation, more disreputable members than any other club, and more "specialists" for the right jobs.

Round, president of the Iron Horsemen

One of them could come up with the right part for a bike or car at a good price. Need to get into a car or building? Need a particular weapon? Need to put the pressure on someone? Need to coerce or lean on someone? Need to make a retaliation? Need a certain kind of entertainment for a party?

They were located not only in Cincinnati but had chapters throughout the country. Their network of communication with their chapters was very effective. They were not the largest motorcycle club in Cincinnati, but they were the baddest. Quality was what they said defined them as the baddest.

The Iron Horsemen, my target outlaw motorcycle club, had heard about me from some of the bikers with whom I had ridden. They had seen me at a distance at different places where bikers gathered. They had read about me in the paper.

I needed an excuse to meet with them. I couldn't just drop in where they met, or at Round's house, for a casual conversation or pastoral visit. They were skeptical of people outside of their own very private circle, especially preachers. Although they knew of me and that I raced motorcycles and rode with the BIA and Cobras, they had no intention of trusting a preacher they didn't know.

I had a run-in with the police while riding with the Cobras and I used that experience as my excuse to meet with the Horsemen. I wanted to use the notion that bikers should get their side of the story in the newspapers instead of always being badmouthed.

One of the Cobras I was close to knew some of the Horsemen. He and I went to the apartment of one of the Horsemen. Three Horsemen were there and he introduced me to them. We sat in the apartment for quite a while and not one of the Horsemen said a word. Through all the silence, I began to feel nervous and intimidated. I began to ask questions that could be answered with a "yes" or "no," but I got only grunts in return. I asked them to call Round and ask him if I could talk to him. After a while, I realized they were stoned and couldn't help me at all. I did manage to get Round's phone number. Before I left, I told them to tell him I would call. To fulfill my pastoral function, I left my card.

When I phoned Round, I was not sure of the response I would get. I expected to get a flat rejection like, "We don't need no preacher around." Instead, he told me to stop over anytime. He said, "Yeah, I remember you. You got the cherry bike with the titty blue grips. I heard about your run-in with the Cobras. Yeah, I would be glad to talk to you about getting something good in the papers about us."

I had all kinds of fears and anxieties about going to his home. I was hoping he would be there alone with his family and we could have a nice casual conversation. I didn't want any confrontational verbiage or attitudes from him and some of the Horsemen who might be there.

When I walked into his living room there were eight Horsemen sitting around. "Let the preacher sit down. Don't be drinkin' any more shit. He's good people. He even wore his damn collar." There was no "Hello, how you doin'?" Everybody just stared at me like I was a big intrusion. After I sat down, I waited for someone to make casual conversation that usually takes place during a pastoral visit. Instead, Round asked, "Now, what was it you wanted, preacher?"

"You already heard I got in trouble a few weeks ago with a couple of cops when I was riding with the Cobras. We did nothing wrong. It was just like some of the stuff you have experienced. We had a good attorney from one of the Methodist Churches here in town. Nothing happened to the cops in spite of our testimony in court and letters from our attorney to the chief of police. We really got screwed. It just made the image of bikers even more negative."

I paused and expected them to nod in agreement with all that I had said. There was no reaction of any kind. I began to feel I was treading on territory where I had no business. I got stone silence. A tall, skinny guy standing in the corner said, "OK, preacher, so what?"

I continued.

"I wanted to know if you would be interested in presenting your side of the story firsthand to the newspapers. It might cool off the cops and it might get the citizens to recognize bikers as human beings." The religion editor of the *Cincinnati Post and Times Star,* James Adams, had done an article about me. I had talked to him about my upcoming visit to the Iron Horsemen and asked if he would help me if I could arrange a meeting for them to tell their story. He had agreed.

Horsemen arrive for Scarface's wedding

Best man at Horseman wedding

The Horsemen listened to me but they didn't seem impressed. Round responded for all of them. (I had learned that the president of a biker club is very much in control as leader and spokesman.) "Who the hell is going to believe us? Al Shottlecotte? He's the biggest news anchor in Cincinnati. He hates our guts. Everybody would just as soon see the cops waste us. It's a good idea, preacher, but there is no way in hell anybody is going to listen to us tell our story."

That was just the comment I needed.

"I've got this friend, James Adams, who is an editor at the *Post and Times Star*. He is the one who did the article about me, 'Minister to the Outlaws.' He said he would be very willing to meet with you and all the Iron Horsemen and write up your side of the story."

Draco Dave spoke up quickly. "For real? You mean we get our names and pictures in the paper with no hassle?"

Farmer John continued on with the prospects of what this could turn out to be by saying, "We could make the front page." That got everybody real excited.

Porky went on to say to no one in particular, "Can you dig it, baby?"

Happy Couple Exchanges Rings
. . . bikers' "chaplain" marries them and buries them

Leader Of Motorcycle Gang Vows 'I Do' In Ault Park

Local paper covered Scarface's wedding

Scarface spoke up next. I considered him one of the most respected and trusted Horsemen. He usually had his girlfriend with him and always treated her with courtesy and respect, which was not usual for most bikers. He seemed always to be thinking. I never saw him act impulsively. Yet, I am not sure how he got the scar across his cheek below his left eye. I performed the wedding service for him and Kay about six months later.

"How do we know we can trust this citizen Adams? How do we know we can trust you? My experience with preachers is not good. Too many times they have tried to save my soul with 'sweet Jesus' shit and denounced me as a lost heathen at the same time." Pointing his finger at me, he said, "What the fuck you getting out of all this, preacher? Round, this could be a setup."

Bride and groom leave for the wedding reception

I started getting hostile looks.

Round seemed pleased to let me squirm while everyone talked with a bit of agitation in their voices. Round settled everybody down. "Preacher, you call this Adams guy, and let us know when and where he wants to talk to us. If he really wants to listen, we will give him something to write. Let us know when he is ready. But, if this is a way to jerk us around, you better keep your ass in Northside and never come out." He used his beer bottle to point me to the door. I knew the conversation was over.

That ended my first meeting with the Iron Horsemen. I felt confident I would be able to gain their trust and help them in many ways. I knew that Jim would do his part to make my ministry to them fruitful. Not only was he interested in doing a unique article for the paper, he was the religion editor of the paper and a devout Christian who was supportive of my ministry to the motorcycle clubs. When the IH met him, they would see how sincere and genuine he was. They would learn that their trust in me and him was well-founded.

I took Jim to Round's apartment to get the groundwork laid for a future meeting with him and the Iron Horsemen. Jim seemed very confident meeting with Round.

I was anxious and nervous. Jim went with the notion that he had something to offer that the Horsemen needed.

He told Round and the other Horsemen who were there, "I am not going to make you out as boy scouts, but I do believe you have a legitimate complaint and I am willing to make your views known. I am wondering, however, if we could go a step further. Instead of saying that you are tired of the hassles with the police and the public, why not provide the public with an idea of what you guys think about life, some discussion of your families, how the Iron Horsemen got started and why, a description of your lifestyle, and something about your individual backgrounds."

Round said, "OK, man, bring your pad and pencil and we will lay it on you." We decided the second meeting would be at the parsonage.

Round notified all the Horsemen and called a "mandatory" at the parsonage. Only an extreme excuse got a member out of a mandatory. Usually, a mandatory was called when a club was going to have a confrontation with another club. Weapons were always carried on a mandatory.

Jim came prepared with pad and pencil and each Horseman came prepared with a bottle or jug of cheap Mogan David wine, the drink of choice at almost every biker meeting and gathering. Before anything was said and after everyone found a place to sit, Round laid out the ground rules.

"We are at the preacher's house, so no cussin'. No smoking. You only drink if the preacher says it's OK. Nobody talks out of turn. You got something to say, raise your hand. Mr. Adams came to hear what we got to say, so don't act like a bunch of jack-asses. He ain't goin' to make us out as saints or boy scouts but we got a chance to make our point. So act like you got some brains. Preacher, can we drink?"

After such a presentation of the ground rules and the respect shown me and my family and home, it was easy to say "yes." Besides, there were twenty-six of them and they were all carrying "iron."

The meeting lasted for over three hours. Jim asked many questions and he listened to them very intently and sincerely. Hands went up often as each one had something he felt had to be said. The more Jim listened, the more they opened up. Jim promised that what they had said would be written up in a thorough and thoughtful way. When the meeting ended, every Horseman shook Jim's hand and genuinely seemed to like him. The meeting was everything I had hoped it would be.

A few days later, the Iron Horsemen made the headlines of the *Cincinnati Post and Times Star.* The story ran two days on page one. The Horsemen were ecstatic.

As soon as the papers hit the street, they were all over the city picking up copies. They drove to the parsonage looking like they were in charge of a paper drive for charity. Their cars were loaded with papers and the guys on bikes had someone ride with them to carry the extras. They joked they were going to "paper Round's apartment." At the parsonage they read the article and celebrated. They said, "We made it big, man. What will all the jags think when they read this?"

My goal was to engage the Iron Horsemen. Now I had accomplished that goal.

I continued to develop a relationship with them that I never had with any other club. They trusted me. I rode with them on several runs. I was invited to their parties. I invited them to appear with me on television talk shows. They went with me to visit my seminary, United Theological Seminary in Dayton, Ohio, at the invitation of one of my professors while I was doing graduate work. They often came to our home and visited and they knew they could call me anytime. I was the only non-member of the Iron Horsemen to sit in on some of their meetings.

I served as their pastor in many ways. I visited them in jail, prison, and hospitals, officiated at weddings, cared for and ministered to their parents and family members, conducted funerals for them and their relatives, and went to court with them. When they had financial problems, I helped get school supplies and clothing for their kids, helped with groceries and gas, and helped with their utilities. I helped them get loans. In these ways and so many more, I was able to introduce them to the grace and love that only Christ can give.

A few clubs wanted to take on the Horsemen to see who would be "king of the hill." In my experience with the bikers from 1969 through 1972, those who tried to dislodge the Horsemen as "king of the hill," never made it. The tactic most of them used was a straight confrontation to find who would be the last man standing. A spokesman from a rival club would call Round and tell him to bring the Horsemen and meet them at a certain place and a certain time. I was privy to this information only twice and both times I got the feeling that no one wanted to take on the Horsemen. The other gang always found excuses not to show up.

The exception to this "I don't want to go" feeling was when a member of the Renegades stole the colors of one of the Horsemen. Every Horseman became incensed with revenge. They surrounded the home of the president of the Renegades and Round shouted to him that he had two minutes to bring out the colors or they would start shooting out the windows, bust the door down, and come in and get them. One of the old ladies of the Renegades brought out the colors.

After that incident, the Renegades slowly ceased to be heard from or seen because they were afraid to wear their colors again. Just like the Avengers, they didn't want to meet a Horseman unexpectedly some place because the Horsemen never called off the war with the Renegades.

The Gladiators used different tactics when they had their war with the Iron Horsemen. They found a Horseman at a bar in Norwood. First, they trashed his bike, and then they went in and told everyone to leave. They used their brass knuckles and chain belts on him. They knew the Horsemen would retaliate so they set a trap for the Horsemen one night at an auto show at the Cincinnati Gardens. The Gladiators did not wear their colors so they would not be identified as a motorcycle club.

The Horsemen came into the Gardens wearing their colors and recognized some of the Gladiators. Identifying six of them, they dragged them into the men's restroom and started using their chain-belts on them. The other Gladiators called the police. When the police came they saw only Iron Horsemen and figured the Gladiators to be citizens. All the Horsemen were arrested for fighting and jailed.

When they were released from jail, they settled the issue by finding each Gladiator and beating him with chain-belts and blackjacks. Just like the Avengers and Renegades, the Gladiators slowly left the biker scene in the Cincinnati area. No outlaw club survived a war with the Iron Horsemen.

During the summer of 1971, dynamite bombings occurred at the homes of Iron Horsemen in Mt. Lookout, Norwood, and Pleasant Ridge. The Horsemen blamed the bombings on a rival group, the Outlaws. Cincinnati police swore out a warrant for the arrest of Gar Hammon, the president of the Outlaws.

Round said that the Outlaws didn't like the Horsemen's attitude about turf boundaries. Round said, "We don't have boundaries. Any place a Horseman sits is Horsemen country; if anyone feels that he doesn't like it, he can try to do something about it. That is what stuck in the craw of Gar Hammon. They didn't like our stand on boundaries. So, they come out to shoot and blow up our houses. I don't operate that way. I'll talk to you first before I shoot you."

With the warrant out for Gar, the bombings stopped. "We don't bomb people's places. We will take individual guys and use a chain because a chain is a respectable weapon. But, the war with the Outlaws is basically over. The funny thing about a war is that it just stops. That's it. It is over. Everything goes back to the way it was before."

Jim Adams reported on one of the wars that took place during the spring of 1970.

He wrote about three bikers from the Lost Children who sauntered into the Seven Sons motorcycle clubhouse in Covington, Kentucky, and asked to join the party.

Before the evening was over, the visitors had pulled a gun, forced the Seven Sons to kneel, and removed their colors.

It was an act of war.

"This is for Oregonia!" the gun-wielding visitors shouted before they left. (The Seven Sons had assisted police against the Lost Children, a hostile Ohio club, during a fracas at a recent hill climb in Oregonia, Ohio.)

Some Lost Children attempted to take one of the Seven Sons along with them but he made a break for it and escaped. A bullet whizzed past him into the clubhouse. The Lost Children roared off.

In another incident, on Thanksgiving Day, it was comparatively quiet in Clermont County, except for a fire that burned down the two-story clubhouse of the Animals.

Arson was suspected.

The Henchmen were also suspected. No complaints were filed by the Animals because motorcycle clubs prefer handling matters their own way. Duke, the president of the Animals, called me and wanted me to set up a meeting with Ace, the president of the Henchmen.

I was very suspicious at that request. The Animals never had a liking for me. They never invited me to ride with them. I could not imagine them asking me to arrange a talk with the president of the Henchmen to resolve the issue of their clubhouse being burned down.

I asked Duke what he had in mind about where, when, and who. He said he wanted the meeting someplace on the eastside, to arrive in a car, with just him and Ace, late one night.

I told him, "I will be present with you and Ace and we will meet someplace in Northside. We will ride bikes, not cars, and we will meet at White Castles during the day." Too often, if clubs showed up someplace in cars, and only a few were to arrive, some guys would hide in the cars. That especially worked best at night. It was always safer and no surprises to be on bikes if the ground rules were, "Nobody else, just one person." Nobody could trust anyone.

When I told Duke my ground rules, he said, "Fuck you, preacher."

"How could you be so ignorant to think I would let you set up Ace? Duke, how about if I meet you anyplace you say on the eastside, alone, just the two of us. I will

help work out peace between you guys and the Henchmen. We could meet in Batavia and I'll buy lunch."

"I'll meet you in hell, you asshole."

Skirmishes continued between the Henchmen and the Animals. One day, when an ex-Animal was staying at the parsonage, Duke and the Animals came and created a disturbance wanting to see him. They were all arrested in front of the parsonage by the Fifth District.

After their clubhouse was burned down and some members became less willing to be at war, the Animals ceased to be an influence or threat to anyone.

Some individual bikers would go out of their way to get into a war with another biker club. There was one Horseman who would never make it as president of a club because everyone knew that if he were elected president, they would always be at war with someone.

One such biker, an Outlaw, almost got the Outlaws and Henchmen into a war. He walked into the Henchmen's meeting place, pulled out two pistols, and told the Henchmen to hand over their colors or they would be at war. One of the Henchmen, in a dumb act of defiance, told him what he could do with his guns and to consider them at war.

When the Outlaw left he began to shoot out the windows of the Henchmen clubhouse.

The president of the Henchmen called the president of the Outlaws and told him they didn't want war but if they kept shooting up their meeting house they would have no choice. The Outlaw president said he did not send the guy over and that they didn't want war either. In this case, one guy just about got two clubs in an all-out war.

I tried to be the reconciler between biker clubs that were at war. It didn't happen often because that was one area in which they didn't want any interference, especially from a preacher. One time I went to the meeting house of one of the Coffin Cheaters to pick up the colors they had stolen from one of the Dracos. "The Dracos sent me over here to talk to you. They don't like the idea that you stole a set of their colors. They sent me here to pick them up and if I don't bring them back, they will come and get them."

The Coffin Cheaters seemed to be in a good mood when they saw me come in the door. After I made my statement, they still seemed to be in the welcome mood. "OK, preacher, here they are. Tell them no hard feelings. Tell them that Spade just got too drunk to know what he was doing."

Another time, I visited the apartment of the president of the Nobody's Children and told him, "Doc wants me to tell you that they want peace. They've invited you to their place Saturday for a party. They said there would be no trouble." The message from the Lost Souls seemed to be accepted since I was the one who brought it. I was glad they trusted me with their messages, because if a biker brought a similar message, they wouldn't know if it was a setup or not. They all knew that I would never be a part of a setup.

Being a member of an outlaw biker club like the Iron Horsemen was very attractive to guys who wanted to join. They wanted to join an outlaw biker club in order to project the image they saw in the Iron Horsemen. They wanted to join because they would feel accepted and have a sense of belonging. They would feel important. They wanted to have the feeling of being powerful, strong, daring, independent, free, and somebody special.

I spoke at one of the Cincinnati high schools about my involvement with the gangs. After the assembly, a few of the students came up to talk to me. In my speech, I talked about characteristics of some of the bikers. I mentioned one member of a club in particular—about how mean, unpredictable, and wild he was and described some of the bizarre things he had done. I mentioned that he was a dropout from one of the city's high schools and had become a very big and powerful member of the club he belonged to. I didn't mention his name or where he had lived in the city or what club he belonged to.

The students who talked to me asked about a former friend of theirs who had dropped out of their school and joined one of the outlaw biker clubs. They wanted to know if I had ever run into him. I asked them to describe him to me.

They said he "is tall and skinny, very quiet and mild mannered, courteous, and the kind of guy who just wouldn't fit into an outlaw biker club."

I asked, "What is his name?"

They mentioned his name and it was the same guy I had talked about in my presentation; wild, mean, and unpredictable. It was Casey. I didn't tell them he was the same guy. I doubt they would have believed me anyway.

How could a person they described go through such a complete and radical change in personality and behavior? It was hard for me to believe that the young man the students asked about was this same hard-nosed, belligerent, big-mouth that I knew. I broke up very few fights between bikers, but he was involved in one fight I broke up.

I stopped the fight when he was beating up a pledge. The other bikers didn't like my interference, but he was getting too close to inflicting serious damage. I pushed him aside and pulled out my hose. He seemed so puny to me when I shoved him aside with my hands on his bony chest. I never considered him a threat at all. He just looked at me and the guy he had beaten. He turned around and walked away. He was a punk. He was not the mild-mannered, courteous guy that his former friends described.

Casey had mentioned to me once that he came from a rotten home situation. He said, "My old man was always drunk and beat my mom, me, and my two brothers and sister."

One of the common questions I asked the bikers was, "Did you ever get any support, encouragement, and affirmation from your parents?"

Casey said he was always told by his dad and mom that he was a nobody and would never amount to anything. Most of the bikers responded with the same answer.

Casey characterized most of the guys who joined an outlaw biker club. They were loners. They never made it in school. They weren't active in their schools and they had very few friends who were active in school. They usually didn't have girlfriends.

Crazy Horse spoke about those who join. "We consider ourselves a minority group. You could consider us a minority because we have been rejected by our parents and most everyone in our families, and by our friends. Most of us have come from broken homes. Most of the guys never had anybody and the club is all they got, so we are just one big family."

Many of those who found the image of an outlaw biker club attractive had low self-images. Before they became members of motorcycle clubs, their self-esteem was symbolized by stooped shoulders, hands stuck deep in their pockets, and heads hung down. They seemed just to drag from one place to another. They seldom were motivated to accomplish anything or contribute to the good of others. Just like Casey, while in school their teachers knew them only as silent, uninvolved persons. They didn't seem to matter to anybody. Especially, themselves.

With all those problems, and with such a negative attitude about himself, a guy like Casey was attracted to a biker club with its activities and publicity. He saw the respect they had because of the colors they wore. He saw them stick their chests out in a pompous kind of way. He saw how they held their heads up in a cocky arrogance. He saw them on their motorcycles, heard the noise, felt the vibrations of the power, and marveled at the attention they got from people. They were nomadic and free and could go anyplace, anytime. They didn't take any crap from anybody. They were in charge. They didn't have to take orders from anybody; they were doing their own thing. They were somebody. A guy like Casey wanted to belong and be a part of that image.

Bikers wanted to project the image of the intimidating power and strength that gladiators did in times past. They wanted to strike fear in people like a horseman wearing iron, or an outlaw of the old west, or the 1920s and 1930s gangster. They wanted people to dread seeing them much like the condemned didn't want to see the dreaded henchman depicted in novels. They wanted to project the rebelliousness of a renegade. They wanted to be brothers armed for anything. They wanted people to realize they could avenge or inflict punishment if that was their wish.

When they got on their choppers and rode with their brothers, the jags looked at them in amazement. They wore the colors of the Henchmen, Devil's Disciples, Satan's Angels, Iron Horsemen, Renegades, Brothers In Arms, Avengers, or Gladiators on their backs. They became somebody. They took pride in being one-percenters; "one for all and all for one." "You cause trouble for one of us, you will have all of us beat your ass." They took pride in being one-percenters also because ninety-nine percent of the bikers in America belonged to the American Motorcycle Association, an organization they had no use for. As one-percenters, they had a strong bond of brotherhood. Nobody would call them a nobody now. They were somebody. That was why they joined.

For once in their lives, they were in charge of their lives. Finally, they were somebody who mattered. Finally, they belonged.

Casey didn't join an outlaw biker club just to become a tough guy. That image and role evolved the longer he associated with his fellow bikers. He joined because he wanted to be accepted and a part of something.

Some guys joined because they wanted to get involved in the hard role, the tough image. Before they joined they were not the Marlon Brando sort portrayed in the movie, *The Wild Ones*. Some were small physically and were tired of being pushed around. Belonging to a biker club, they would have an image of authority, brawn, power, and they would be willing to fight back. A Henchman told me, "Nobody messes with us when we wear our colors."

CHAPTER FOUR

There were many other reasons why guys joined outlaw biker clubs. One guy joined a club after his wife threw him out of the house and his brother-in-law told him never to come back again. He started living with a member of the Satan's Sinners and took on the role of a tough guy. He bought a chopper and started riding with the Satan's Sinners. No one was ever going to throw him out of anyplace again.

It was interesting to hear former friends and family members describe those who joined the biker clubs so they could become identified as tough guys. A girl who lived across the street from one of the toughest Iron Horsemen told me what he was like when he was growing up. "He was kind of a mama's boy and always stuck around home. He always avoided trouble and fights; that just wasn't him. And now, when I hear about him getting locked up for fighting and doing all the crazy things he does, he isn't fooling me at all. He just hasn't grown up."

I found that other bikers fit that same mold. They had been spoiled all their lives and always had things given to them. Once they got older and found that their employers, girlfriends, wives, in-laws, teachers, parents, friends, and society wouldn't continue to cater to their every whim, they acted out. They would get loud, abusive, and go into a rage. One could call it a major temper tantrum. An outlaw motorcycle club was the ideal place for them to act out this behavior.

The immature leave-me-alone anger was the same outburst the Brothers In Arms yelled at me when I was trying to break up the fight between them and the Gladiators, "Don't touch us, man! Nobody touches us!"

The attitude of having it their own way cost many of them their marriages, families, and jobs. "Take this job and shove it," would have been a great theme song for them.

One of the Stallions was told by his boss at one of the department stores downtown to cut his hair. He took great pride in telling me and the other Stallions, "I told him to stick the job up his ass." He walked off and never went back.

An Iron Horseman was told not to wear his colors to work. He, too, walked off.

Very few of the Brothers In Arms, Cobras, Henchmen, or others had regular full-time jobs because they didn't want anybody telling them what to do. With only a few exceptions did any of the bikers have a full-time job. Many of them took part-time jobs when they were pushed to come up with some money. Many took unemployment, stole tools, bikes, and parts off bikes and cars to sell them.

The Dracos had a unique way of making money. They came to me one day and offered me a beautiful console record player. They said, "This will really look great in your living room. It will only cost you fifty bucks."

I asked how come it was so cheap.

They said, "We have a truckload of them in that truck parked out in the street. Take your pick." I didn't know much about hot merchandise, but I never took the beautiful console record player.

The attitude that drew many to an outlaw biker club, that kept them out of school, and that kept them from holding a job, also didn't help when some of them joined the military because they would soon be on the streets, AWOL. Many of them verbalized often, "We are free and independent. We don't need anybody. Nobody tells us what to do. We don't have to answer to anybody. The world stinks, so we are going to do our own thing." From 1969 through 1972, I found there was no better place to live out that twisted view of life, than with outlaw bikers. That's why they joined. They wanted to make a name for themselves and have somebody take notice.

Some joined for more superficial reasons. The television series, "Then Came Bronson," added to the popularity of the biker clubs. Bronson portrayed another hero doing his own thing, being independent, not tied to any of the expectations, requirements, or regulations of the cultural norm. He further enhanced their image. He rode a Harley, wore a black leather jacket, jeans, boots, and a black stocking cap. He was his own boss, never had to answer to anyone, seemed always to have problems with the law, and had plenty of ladies who wanted to ride off into the sunset with him.

The popular movie *Easy Rider* added to the mystique and glamour. They believed belonging to a biker club was where all the action was—chicks, booze, drugs, fights, bars, sex parties, choppers, the power from wearing the colors, and the power of riding down the street while everyone looked at them in awe.

Round said that some who joined the Iron Horsemen were real wack-jobs. They had psychological problems, but at the beginning of their membership with the IH, they fit in very well with their crazy antics. But, killing someone for no apparent reason was out of character even to them.

I visited the jails to see bikers who were in for murder. Some of the killings took place, not because they were trying to fulfill the role of tough guy in the club, but because they were mentally ill. Even the most notorious outlaw clubs weeded out the sickos once they found out what these guys were like.

A member of the IH shot a young man after a movie on the sidewalk near the theater in front of several people, simply because the young man laughed at a particular comment made in the movie. The Horseman explained in court, in a very nonchalant way, that he shot him because he laughed at the wrong time. The court recommended that the Horseman receive psychiatric treatment with his fifty-year prison sentence. Round said they dropped him from the club. "We are not going to go out of our way to create trouble for anybody."

Crazy Horse told an *Enquirer* reporter: "I've got my own ideas about prospects. I'll never jack around with a prospect. My opinion of a prospect when he comes into the club is that they have a bike and they get out there and ride that bike and they act like a brother to you. I have seen a lot of good people and I've seen a lot of jerks. I have spent three years in the Horsemen trying to get rid of all these jerks we've got in the club, and I think we've done a good job of it. I can't stand to see a wise punk come into the club just because he has a patch on his back. Bike clubs are something you better think twice about before you go into it. There's more to it than just bumming around on the bikes."

One such young man wanted to join the Dracos. One of the Dracos told me about him, "He had a wise mouth and could not get it together at all and not too many of the brothers cared for him. We tried to tell him he was not ready for this kind of life. His heart was not in it for one thing. He was doing it for a showboat basis so he could be around us at the bars, drink beer and stuff, have a lady hanging on his arm, and wear colors and impress people. That's the whole reason he wanted to come in.

"That is not what it is all about. He didn't get voted in. He joined another club. I don't want to mention which one, but he did the same thing with them that he did with us. He won't last with them either."

Others joined because they were all mixed-up and confused about life, who they were, and where they were going. They had no direction for their lives and would attach themselves to almost anything.

Others joined because they were in a rock-bottom depression. Some had a girlfriend or wife walk out on them. Some got fired from their jobs, thrown out of school, or homes. Others got caught up in a sick and hopeless concept of life.

The field was ripe for harvest. How would they hear without a preacher?

The years 1969 through 1972 was a time that made joining an outlaw motorcycle club very attractive. There may have been no other time when so many motorcycle clubs existed. The movie *The Wild Ones*, with Marlon Brando in the early 50s, provided the impetus outlaw bikers needed. In greater Cincinnati, during those three years, I encountered twenty-six biker clubs.

The late 60s and early 70s were very turbulent times and were characterized by a different attitude among young adults. The times created Timothy Leary, Allen Ginsberg, Jerry Rubin, Abbie Hoffman, Eldridge Cleaver, the Grateful Dead, LSD, flower children, the Student Nonviolent Coordinating Committe, the Students for Democratic Society, the New Left, Yippies, Hippies, Jimmy Hendrix, Janis Joplin, Jim Morrison, the Fugs, other acid-rock stars, and Woodstock.

In their book *Acid Dreams,* Martin A. Lee and Bruce Shlain wrote:

> *If any single theme dominated young people in the 1960's, it was the search for a new way of seeing, a new relation to the world. When the social fabric starts to unravel, as it did in the late 1960s, the fabric of the psyche also unravels. People needed to put their lives back together and regain their sanity after the turmoil of those years. For some this meant going off to live in a commune or farm in the country where they could wage a revolution of purely private expectations. Others took solace in Eastern swamis.*

Some joined outlaw biker clubs.

Some outlaw biker clubs were fearsome and some were just wannabes. Some had just a half-dozen members and some had more. Some had been around for more than two years, some never lasted two months. Some had charismatic, strong leaders; some did not have any leadership at all. Some had regular meeting houses and some just met in bars or someone's home or apartment. Some had rules, regulations, and by-laws, and some just flew by the seat of their pants. Some rode only Harley choppers, some rode on anything and any size. Some were part-timers, some seven days a week, twenty-four hours a day.

Not everybody made it into membership of an outlaw biker club. A pledge for most of the outlaw clubs had to go through an almost impossible, difficult initiation/testing period.

One of the Horsemen said, "You have at least thirty days as a prospective member; some have gone as a prospect as long as four or five months. If there is a person who can't get it together, then he is thrown out. We don't screw around like we used to."

Another Horseman said, "When we get a guy who is going to come into our chapter, we will not allow any of our solid members to do anything unjust to the pledge; and if the pledge is told to do something stupid, the member is going to have to do it, too. We don't stand for any member to beat up on another who is going to be your brother. Someday your life may depend on him."

The length of the probation period varied with different clubs, but it was usually four weeks. Each club had its own rules and practices for each pledge to go through before he was voted into the club as a full member. During the pledging period, he wore only the top rocker of the colors with the bottom half added once he had successfully finished his probation.

The requirements of the IH were that a pledge had to be at least eighteen and must have a Harley Davidson motorcycle. They preferred that a pledge be twenty-one, but with the legal age at eighteen, they would take an eighteen year old. As Farmer John said, "We will take them if we think they can take it. You can look in their eyes and see if they are serious. If they say 'O, wow, the Iron Horsemen,' we just tell them to hit the road."

With some of the clubs, the requirements of a pledge were unusual, outlandish, and sometimes grotesque.

The expectations of some of the clubs of their pledges were far more crazy and difficult than the immature nonsense I went through as a pledge at Theta Delta Chi at the University of Illinois.

Some of those tasks ranged from drinking from a boot filled with the urine of several bikers, to providing a girl for a train (several guys having sex with her) for the club. Almost anything that was ridiculous was usually something the pledge had to do. When a group of bikers got boozed up, a lot of those things got ridiculous. With some clubs, if a pledge did not do all he was told to do, he got kicked around and beaten before he got blackballed by the club.

It was disgusting when I would hear a pledge tell me how outta sight every-body thought he was when he did some dumb thing he was told to do. Lurch, a prospective pledge of the Horsemen, told me with great pride that an active told him he "really had balls to do all he had done." When he went on and on about how he showed his guts, I asked him, "What would your parents, grandparents, and family think of you doing all that dumb stuff? What do you think I think about it?"

He answered, "I don't give a shit what they think. And, I really don't give a shit what you think. You are nothing but a goddamn holy roller."

Once a pledge makes it through the hazing, he finally belongs. He has shown that he can do almost anything, and he usually has. The more grotesque the nonsense and the more enthusiasm he shows for it, the more respect he gets in the eyes of the members.

He especially earns more respect if he fights for and with his brothers as a pledge. The wilder the fights, the more pain he inflicts on others, the more reckless abandon he demonstrates, the more he enhances his chances of making membership into the club, and the more he becomes someone special.

That even included challenging me to a fight. When pledges tested me that way, it was always the worst of any test I encountered. They had to impress the brothers and their fellow pledges. They were usually drunk or strung out on dope or just plain stupid and immature. They had made it to this level, and to get to the next, they had to do something really mindless. Challenging a preacher to a fight was just that.

At the infamous chili parlor on Calhoun, I was sitting at a table with three other Satan's Angels and next to us was a table with four others. The president was sitting at the counter facing us with a pledge next to him and another Angel on the other side of the pledge. The pledge, wanting to earn some points with his future brothers, said to me for his brothers to hear, "Preacher, let's go outside, I want to see what you got underneath that collar."

He got up from his stool at the counter and before he took a step, I grabbed him by his shoulder, spun him around, and slammed him down on the stool with his back pinned against the counter. I put my hand around his throat and he grabbed it with his right hand. My mouth was right next to his ear and our forheads were touching and I whispered to him, "Don't try to be a tough guy with me. It would be nothing for me to pound you right here in front of everybody. Don't be an immature stupid ass. Now, you walk out of here real civil-like and I want to hear your bike and you better be on it. If you want to see what I am like under my collar, come to the house. You know where I live. Just call me. But, don't ever pull this crap again." He left.

Hawk, their president, and the other Angels who were there, just sat there. Hawk said, "Well, he won't be around anymore. You weeded out another one for us, preacher."

I was at a party with three different biker clubs one evening along the Greater Miami River. Pledges were there, and when so many active club members are present there are many opportunities to make the pledges go through all kinds of foolishness. I never liked being around pledges because most of them did not know me, trust me, or accept me as did most of the bikers I knew. I always felt at risk around them. They were always put in no-win situations by some of the active members.

One biker said to another, "I bet our pledges can eat more shit than yours."

Another said, "I bet we got a pledge who can ride his bike farther into the river than any pledge you got."

One of the presidents asked one of his pledges, "Did you ever kick the ass of a preacher?" I stood there frozen, waiting. I had no business being there in the first place, but a member of the Nomads was leaving for the army in a few days and he asked me to join them. Maybe this question and possible confrontation would end if I let on I wasn't listening. I turned, looked aside, and started walking away.

The pledge answered, "No, I never have."

"Would you like to?"

"Sure." What else would he say?

I was hoping the subject would drop as if it was all a practical joke. It wasn't a dare so maybe the president would laugh it off. I had not ridden with this particular club. I had only met them at rallies with other clubs. I was hoping someone from the Nomads or Coffin Cheaters would intervene.

I knew it was getting out of hand when the president called after me to get my attention. "Hey, preacher."

He told the pledge, "He's the preacher." I was hoping everybody would start laughing and then bring up something else with which to harass the pledges. The president continued his stupid game by saying, "If you got any balls, let's see you kick the preacher's ass."

The pledge approached me with a beer bottle in his hand. He had a look on his face like he didn't know what to do next. I had not used my hose much but I immediately took it out of the back of my jacket. I felt I was in a corner and needed to get out. If I hit the pledge in front of all these bikers, I couldn't predict what they would do because I didn't know anybody from this club. I was afraid the pledge would become a maniac in retaliation since I showed him up. But, I was not going to back down to such senseless, imbecilic behavior.

"You take one more step toward me and you will have to be hauled home. I've never heard or seen so much stupid and immature bullshit in my life. You try

"Deacon" of the Coffin Cheaters

anything and you and everyone else here won't be going to anymore parties." I looked at the president and said, "I've had it with your stupid nonsense."

I was ready, prepared, and even hoping to use the hose, when Deacon, the sergeant in arms of the Coffin Cheaters said, "Leave the preacher alone. He's good people. You see that hose in his hand? I've seen him use it before. If the preacher hits you with that hose, you will wish you hadn't shown up here. Now, back off and leave him alone."

Deacon then said something to the president of the pledge. I didn't hear what it was he said. Deacon turned to me and told me to ride on home. I was glad he stepped in, but I was kind of curious what would have happened had I hit that fat punk pledge. I am afraid I would have come out on the short end of such a fight. Nevertheless, I left at that moment and was glad to make the ride home.

For some reason, none of the bikers who joined an outlaw club ever considered that there was no retirement plan. That was when I discovered a new and difficult pastoral function I was going to have with them. When a biker joined, it was for life. Some of them didn't think of that. Or, if they did, they didn't realize that when they dropped out they were making a very serious and dangerous decision.

Trashcan had gone to the motorcycle race to watch his brother, whom I had raced against. I was also racing that day and happened to see Trashcan in the pit area. He gave me a nod of recognition before the race began, but it was not until the second heat that he came by to say hello. I sensed a bit of hesitation when he came up to see me. He seemed embarrassed. He didn't look like the old Trashcan I knew from the Iron Horsemen. He was wearing a t-shirt, jeans, wasn't wearing colors, his hair was short, he didn't have a beard, and was he wearing gym shoes.

After we said our hellos, I asked him about the Horsemen. He said he had dropped out a while back and then he quickly changed the subject. What he said and how he said it was a big contrast to the usual way bikers speak of their commitment to their colors and allegiance to each other.

Once, at the parsonage, a minister friend of mine asked Trashcan how tight the Iron Horsemen were. My friend asked him, "I heard that most of you bikers have a motto, 'one for all and all for one.' Is that true?"

Trashcan began to pontificate, "The brothers are so close, nothing can separate us. We are willing to die for each other. We have this thing for each other that we are one and that we will drop what we are doing and go to a brother in need at any time, under any circumstances. Now you show me a church member who will do that for any member of his church. We know each other and we consider each other a brother. Can you say that for everyone in your church? Hell, no you can't. And some church members hate each other's guts while they sit in the pews on Sunday morning."

When Trashcan told me he dropped out of the Horsemen, I wondered if he remembered that day at the parsonage when he told my friend how tight the Horsemen were. Where was that deep commitment now? What happened to change all that? What about that image he so desperately wanted to show that he was tough, to be feared, and never had a care?

Before he went over to his brother's bike to load up and leave for home, I asked him. "I never knew of a Horseman or any biker dropping out of his club. Why did you?" He kept looking over his shoulder toward his brother, as if he had to leave and help pack up. He finally looked at me and said, "I had enough. I just grew up. I didn't need the game anymore. I found out that I can be a man without the colors and the bike. I don't need to play the role anymore. Skip, I just grew up." The way he said it was like it was a bad experience he just wanted to forget.

He told me he rode over to Round's house to tell him he was dropping out. He didn't realize what he was getting into by dropping out. He had heard rumors and he had seen what happened to some former bikers when they dropped out. But, he thought he had a special relationship to Round and some of the others. He didn't figure they would give him a hard time.

When he approached Round to give back his colors, there were a few other Horsemen there. They ripped off his colors and beat him with his own chain-belt. They drove him over to his girlfriend's house and dumped him in her yard. They messed his bike up so badly he couldn't sell it for much except junk and parts.

When I had a conversation with Round several months earlier, I asked him, "What happens when a brother leaves the Horsemen?"

He said, "Whenever anybody leaves the Horsemen, they better stay clear of us for a long time."

"Skip, I just grew up." What wonderful words to hear! But, Trashcan was the only one to ever tell me that.

Another great phrase I heard was from Gypsy. He said, "I didn't want to go through anymore stupid shit." Making it through the probation period and a few weeks of membership may have fulfilled some senseless need at the time, but Gypsy, a former member of the Fugueros, found out that he was trying to be someone he wasn't.

I met him when I got together with the Fugueros for rides and occasional outings. When he was considering dropping out he came to the house and told me he had had it. He said he was going to leave the Fugueros and go to St. Louis to live with his uncle for a while. After things cooled off, he wanted to come back to live with his mom and get a job. He said he wanted to tell his story to young people so they wouldn't make the same mistakes he made.

When he came back to Cincinnati, he came back to see me. He got acquainted with Filthy and they went along with me to some speaking engagements at churches and schools. His story was, "I had two years of college, I dropped out, joined a rock band, went to work in California, traveled all over the country, drove a beer truck, and finally ended up with the Fugueros. I was searching for myself like a lot of mixed-up people do. I tried everything but nothing satisfied me. I was stupid enough to try all kinds of jigs. I heard the preacher say more than once, at a funeral or something, 'Not many of us have the guts to look Jesus square in the face. It will cost us too much. We will have to stop and listen and think.'

I finally stopped all the stupid stuff I was doing. I was going nowhere. Doing nothing. I stopped and listened and began to think. I saw Filthy Phil hangin' out at the preacher's house and, man, did he do a turn-around. I was going to, too. So, Filthy and me go out with the preacher sometimes to visit his people. We even went to some of the nursing homes with him. Talk about freakin' people out. We don't wear any colors, we don't have any. We just don't look too good. But we teased them, talked to them, and Skip prayed. It was fun. I am living with my mom now and we are getting along just fine. Filthy and me are working at it and we will make it."

When Filthy Phil dropped out of the Brothers In Arms, he left town for about two weeks. When he came back, he avoided his former brothers. He knew what would happen. Filthy Phil and Cherokee both dropped out about the same time.

They both left Cincinnati and went different ways. When they came back, I put them up at the parsonage until things cooled down.

I told Trashcan to come to the house and stay awhile. He told me he was staying with his brother and his wife. His brother had gotten him a job where he worked. Trashcan did come to the house often to visit. He was convinced he had done the right thing. I just wanted to provide him support and encouragement. He began to gain a sense of confidence in his decision to leave the Horsemen and he began to gain confidence in himself. My family and the church family always made Trashcan feel welcome and at home. I continued to see him and his brother at the motocross races and offered to provide help anyway I could. Trashcan's brother and his brother's wife had done so much for him and they were letting him see what family was really all about.

There was a new upstart, wannabe biker club called the Born Losers. Of course, they would gather in Clifton on Calhoun Street where everybody else was. It was easy to see that they were new. They rode mostly 250cc Yamahas and Hondas. Their colors looked like they just bought them from Gold Circle. The colors did not have a sophisticated embroidered emblem; someone, or each of them, used some paint or ink of some sort to draw a distorted face of a man with a knife clutched in his teeth and a fist next to the face. Those who had boots had new boots. Some wore khaki pants instead of the usual dirty worn jeans. Their bikes were new or a used assortment of colors and makes.

I was making my rounds on the street one day, wearing my suit and collar, when I encountered the Born Losers for the first time. I could tell right away they were new at the game. Not only did they look it, but nobody was hanging with them; they were by themselves, not even a dozen. They saw me and approached me. Even wannabes knew me.

"Hey preacher, how you doin'? You don't know us, but we are the Born Losers." It was just like the start of a conversation with some people when all they want to do is talk about themselves. And, they did.

One of them, whom I took to be their leader, started the recording I had heard dozens of times. "We got it all together. The brothers are righteous. ("Righteous" was biker jargon which does not mean anything in religious terms; it only means "good." Like the bike is "righteous.") We got all kinds of plans. We got a truckload of 74s (another bit of jargon which means motorcycles and parts) from an army camp in Kentucky and we can get them for under two hundred dollars each." This was another part of the recording I had heard at least half a dozen times. Everybody was going to get a shipment of 74s from an army camp in Kentucky and sell them for big bucks.

The recording continued. "We are going to do our own thing and nobody will get in our way. When people see our colors, they are going to be flat torked out of shape. We are going to take no shit from nobody."

I was going to tell him that I had heard the same story from about a dozen clubs and none of them lasted six months. Instead, I said, "You are only heading for trouble. You better just forget about being Born Losers and start thinking about being somebody special. You can't be somebody special if you are in prison where several bikers I know have ended up. I also buried others because they got caught up in the very game you want to play. Get out of this before it is too late. Let's go someplace where we can talk about this."

His response was the one I had heard so many times, "Fuck you, preacher."

It was interesting that Round turned counselor when I encountered wannabes and I failed to get them to stop being outlaw bikers. I told Round, "I met the Born Losers and I tried to convince them not to go any further but they wouldn't listen to me."

He said, "You failed again, huh, preacher? Want me to talk to them? I'll take Cutter with me and we'll scare the hell out of them and rip their colors to shreds. We got too many clubs the way it is."

I had six dropout bikers stay at the parsonage during the course of their hiding out from the gangs they used to belong to. Filthy Phil, Cherokee, Wade, Flake, Cisco, and Mouth. The most at any one time staying at the parsonage was two. The longest stay was one week. This underground haven was in operation from January 1970 to May of 1971. My kids and I referred to the operation we set up as a safe place or a safe house. None of the six referred to the parsonage as a safe place or safe house. That would have been out of character; a former motorcycle gang member needing a safe place? We had plenty of room at the parsonage. A few members of the church knew of the arrangement and those who did were very supportive and very helpful.

I had a small cadre of women bringing in meals whenever we needed them during those seventeen months. The six former bikers provided me with built-in babysitters. When repairs were needed in the house, that was taken care of. When it was time for cleanup, they knew that was one of the expectations. They did their own laundry. They would help get the meals on the table since the kids were in school and I was working. They knew they were not there for a free ride. They had assignments. I required that one book be read. If not read by the time they left, it had to at least be started. It had to come from my bookshelf which left them limited choices.

They were not to leave the house, but I guessed that when I was gone, they might have. It was too risky for them to be out on the streets for any length of time. The six didn't have transportation anyhow. They knew it would be too dangerous for them to go to the several old hangouts which included Clifton, Calhoun, Ludlow, State Avenue, the Broken Drum, and any place in Northside. They knew it was best to just stay put for a few days. Mrs. Wilheit, Mrs. Smith, Mrs. Waldkamp, Mrs. Lambing, Paul Zentgraf, and others from the church saw it as a form of ministry to help mend the bodies, hearts, minds, spirits, and souls of these young men. And, their company and cooking put that ministry in place.

During the time the six dropouts were staying at the parsonage, we occasionally heard the sound of Harleys stopping in front of the house or roaring down Chase Avenue. The sound of bikers arriving wasn't a guarantee that we were going to have a social call. We had to watch out for the arrival of a club of one of the dropouts looking for revenge.

Late one night, six Henchmen rode up in the drive with a lot of noise and stepped up to the front door. They didn't ring the doorbell, they pounded on the door. When they saw me through the glass, they yelled, "Is Cisco in there?"

I told them, "Get off the porch or I will call the police." Cisco was there and I knew what his former fellow Henchmen wanted. They had not "settled" with Cisco. Every time I had a visit like that from a club, they knew I would not turn over their former brother. But, they had to make an appearance. They had to let him know they were poised.

The Animals really hated Flake. He threw his colors in the Ohio River when he crossed the I-75 bridge. I had become good friends with Flake through his mother. She was an emergency room nurse at Christ Hospital and treated me when I had a racing injury. When she found out I knew her son, and how I knew him, she continued to keep in touch with me and said she would join me in my prayers for her son. She visited us at the parsonage and brought meals while Flake was staying there. She also provided us with some wonderful homemade bread even after Flake left to go on his own.

One night when Flake was at our safe house, several of the Animals came by on their bikes to draw him out. They had been drinking. They began to yell, using obscene words, waking up the neighbors, revved up their motorcycle engines, rode into our neighbor's yard, urinated in the church lawn, and created such a disturbance my children became afraid. Flake was the only dropout there. He had been there only three days.

I knew it wouldn't be long before the Fifth District police arrived. I stepped out on the porch and talked to Duke, the president of the Animals, "You are never going to see Flake. You are all going to be behind bars and Flake will be out working, riding, and having a great time. He has more brains in his thumbnail than you jerks have in all your heads put together. Duke, if you want to see Flake, you call me and let me know when you want to come over. I will be with him when you come. Nobody else comes, just you. But, right now, you better get out of here before the police get here."

The police arrived in three squad cars before the Animals left. Flake came out of the house and stood on the porch. As the police began to approach the Animals, Duke, the president said to them, pointing to Flake, "We come to talk to our brother, man. We're not causin' no trouble." The police lined them up facing the wall of the driveway between the church and the parsonage. The police were going through all their pockets and cuffing them. I walked over to Slick, who was one of the youngest of the Animals. He was a good friend of Flake and I got to know him when I stopped over at Flake's house. I came up to him as he was being frisked and cuffed. I told him, "I can fix it with these cops for you to stay here with Flake and me. Give it up and stay here with us. Let me help."

"Fuck you, preacher!"

There were all kinds of reasons for a biker to leave his club. One of the biggest reasons I found was that a biker eventually had to put up or shut up. It was a case of some bikers talking the talk, but not being able to walk the walk.

That was the case of Gunner of the Satan's Sinners. Gunner got shot in the stomach by a rival gang. Before the shooting, he always talked tough about what he would do if he was ever challenged by another outlaw biker or an enraged citizen. He talked the talk.

When I visited him at the hospital, his condition was getting worse and I could tell he was wondering if it was all worth it. I played the devil's advocate and told him, "Your brothers must be pretty proud of you the way you stood your ground and didn't back down from the gun fight." I knew he hadn't shown any guts during the fight. Instead, he was trying to talk his way out of the confrontation. I wanted to see if he was still going to continue the hard act.

"I don't give a shit what they think; they can take my colors and shove em'. I'm getting out. I'm going to lose two or three months of work because of this."

Close calls like Gunner's made several bikers reconsider the cost of playing the role of an outlaw biker. They began to realize what was really important to them. In

Gunner's case, it was his job. Too many times it was too late. I wasn't able to convince them of the foolishness of what they were doing, that their behavior was irresponsible and immature, or that what they were doing was never good or helpful to them or anyone else. I felt helpless and sad at the number who were killed or permanently injured because they were into the role of an outlaw biker.

This was particularly the case with the demise of the Nomads. They talked the talk, but, when it came time to walk the walk, they faltered. Six came storming into my house one night and said, "Sam threw us out of his place tonight and we are going back to burn it down."

Sam's was one of the local bars in Northside near Colerain Avenue. I asked them, "Why did he throw you out?"

"We got in a fight with one of the jags there."

"Well, what do you expect? Of course, he is going to throw you out."

LeRoy slammed his fist down on my desk and said, "Nobody does that to a Nomad."

"If you go down there and pull a stupid stunt like burning his place down, I am going with you and I am going to put a match in your gas tanks. Act like you got some brains in your head. If you cause any trouble for Sam, I will call the cops and you won't ride a bike for a long time."

I knew they were just talking the talk. Why didn't they just go ahead and burn the place down instead of coming to the parsonage to see me and tell me about it? They were just talking the talk. The Nomads were wannabes. They liked the image and they got a lot out of it, to a certain extent. But, when it came time to walk the walk, they needed a preacher to talk them out of it. It was as if they wanted me to be a parent to them.

I began to see the thread that held some of the guys in the Nomads unravel. Their commitment to their colors was very fragile, weak, and shaky. It wasn't long before the Nomads ceased to exist. Mouth dropped out early on and came to the house and was one of the six we took in. None of the Nomads gave him a hassle. Grease left Cincinnati and found a job in Toledo. Bear, who had some serious conflicts with his wife, grew up and renewed his roles of husband and father.

As I mentioned earlier, there was no retirement policy when a biker joined an outlaw club. When they eventually wanted to get out, they wanted a clear, easy, and no-hassle retirement plan. Many times a judge came along with just the right excuse—their out. He would tell them, as they stood before him, "Either you get out of this gang or you go to jail." When they were placed on probation or on parole, they were told, "No more wearing of the colors and no more association with the club." Some felt relief at that condition.

Some Brothers In Arms were told in court, "You have a choice, the workhouse for nine months, or the army." The Vietnam War was going on and many joined the army but were AWOL in Northside even before they had finished basic training. Many of those who went before the judge and were told not to wear their colors again, never went back to the biker club. The time spent away from the outlaw element seemed to dampen their need and interest in getting involved with their biker brothers again.

It was my hope and prayer, and so much a part of my follow-up ministry, that when a biker left that world, he would enter a new life of hope with all kinds of possibilities open to him. I wanted to help nurture him in a spiritual journey that would inspire him and to help him realize new opportunities to experience God's grace. I wanted him to have his spirit lifted from being lost and downcast, to being excited and enthusiastic about what lay ahead for him.

The two men on the road to Emmaus were lost and downcast. The Message explains in Luke's Gospel, 24:13–32, that after the crucifixion, the two men on the road to Emmaus "just stood there, long-faced, like they had lost their best friend."

So many of the bikers who left their clubs needed a boost to their spirits. When the ex-bikers returned home to families, friends, and work, they had a chance to begin a new way of life. They no longer had that brotherhood and lifestyle that they thought would make their lives meaningful. I wanted to help them feel what the two men who encountered Jesus on the road to Emmaus felt. "They didn't waste a minute. They were up and on their way back to Jerusalem." There was hope that their lives had been restored. I wanted to help those former bikers to experience that sense of hope. "Didn't we feel *on fire* as he conversed with us on the road, as he opened up the Scriptures for us?"(emphasis mine).

The NUMC did so much to enable those six dropouts and so many others to see and feel the fire of God's love. It was very rewarding to share the message of Christ to those who would listen, especially those who used the parsonage as a safe place.

CHAPTER FIVE

An article was written about my ministry to the outlaw motorcycle clubs in the *Cincinnati Post and Times Star* in January 1971. It was entitled, "Minister to the Outlaws." I sent the article and two others to Bill Garrett of the Board of Evangelism of the United Methodist Church. The two other articles were about a murder and a gang war that was going on involving the Iron Horsemen.

I made presentations to the Board of Evangelism of the United Methodist Church twice in 1969 in Nashville, Tennessee. Another time, I met with Bill and others from the board in September of 1969 in Washington, D.C. The board was becoming more interested in ways they could help. Bill wanted to come to Cincinnati to visit with me to find out more. Prior to his visit he wrote, "Those news stories were really bad news. Does all of this have any repercussions on you? I hope you don't have to send any more items like the last two."

He wanted to go where the clubs met and meet some of the bikers. He wanted to find out if their war and involvement in the recent murder would have any fallout on me. The person I wanted him to meet was Round. I wasn't sure how Round would take to becoming acquainted with another minister. Especially, a minister from the denominational headquarters.

I felt I may be pushing my luck too far with Round. Just a few weeks before, I invited six different clubs to send a representative to a meeting at the parsonage. I wanted to find out what they thought about my going to churches and schools to talk about my ministry to them. Round sent Farmer John to represent the Horsemen. They told me that speaking about my ministry to them was not a problem. At the meeting, they all said, in one way or another, "Call it like you see it."

I wasn't sure how Round would respond when I told him that Bill wanted to meet him and some of the other Horsemen. Would he be thinking, *Look, we have been tolerating you and giving you lots of latitude. We okayed you talking about us at churches and schools. Now you want us to meet some big-shot church jag?*

I called him and said that Bill wanted to meet him.

Round asked, "What does he want?"

"All he wants is to meet you and some of the other Horsemen. He is afraid that I may be getting into some dangerous territory because of the war going on and the murder that took place. He just wants some assurance I'm not going to get hurt."

"What the hell did you tell him about us?"

Round and I had gotten to a somewhat relaxed place with each other where I could tease him and he would tease me. I said, "I told him you are a pack of animals, that the Horsemen, socially and politically, are just right of Hitler."

There was silence on the other end of the line. I thought I had overstepped my boundaries of teasing. Round finally said, "When he gets in town, let me know and we will get together. Do we have to watch our language?"

When we met Round, I introduced Bill as my boss. Round never shook his hand. He just sat in a big, dirty, worn easy chair in the corner of the bar where they had been meeting. Round always wore tiny oval sunglasses with very thin wire frames. He was a big man and the sunglasses were his way of saying, "You can see a lot of me, but you will never get to know me." His black hair always looked greasy as if he wanted it to match the greasy look of his colors. He was about thirty, but couldn't grow a thick beard. It was scraggy and looked like it was always three or four days old.

Bill realized that small talk was not going to happen. There were about twenty other Horsemen standing around, sitting at some of the tables, or leaning against the bar looking on. Round didn't say anything. He just looked at Bill through those dark sunglasses. No one offered us a chair. Bill looked down at him and asked, so that all the other Horsemen could hear, "What do you and the other Iron Horsemen think of Skip being around?"

"Oh, some of the guys get uptight when he shows his face," Round said. "But they don't run it on him too hard. He's been a big help to us, especially when he wears his collar. Right now it might be good for him if he cooled it with us for a while, but I don't know. Things are getting pretty hot right now and we might need him to wear his collar. I don't ever get in his face. As long as I say he can come around, it's OK."

Before Bill left to go back to Nashville, he suggested to Dr. Brown that a steering committee be set up to assist me when I faced serious issues like he had encountered in his visit to the Iron Horsemen.

Soon after his visit, Cincinnati District Program Director Faye Flint established a steering committee with Dr. Emerson Colaw from the Hyde Park Community United Methodist Church as chairperson. The steering committee consisted of two members of the Northside United Methodist Church, Jewel Smith and Barb Lambing; Rev. Vic Frederickson of Christ Episcopal Church, who had experience working with street gangs in New York City; owner of Western Hills Honda Herschel Benkert, serving as an advisor; Bernie Evanshine who raced motorcycles; James Hey, a patrolman from the Third District of the Cincinnati Police Department; Brother Theodore from the Franciscan Friary; Faye Flint and John Collins, staff persons who represented the district and conference; Leonard Slutz, who was the attorney for the committee and a member of the Hyde Park Community United Methodist Church; Miss Bobbie Stinson, who served as secretary and was a member of State Avenue United Methodist Church; and Rev. Mark Dove of Friendship United Methodist Church. Bill Garrett would attend the monthly meetings when he could, as well as Rod Barr from the New York City office of Urban Young Adult Action.

The purpose of the committee was to provide me with guidance through the labyrinth of legal questions, procedures of what to do with information that bikers entrusted to me, and problems or demands posed by bikers and their families. The committee would also help fund the ministry.

The first meeting of the steering committee met on November 5, 1969. The minutes recorded by the secretary, Bobbie Stinson are as follows:

The first meeting of the Steering Committee for Gene Skipworth met at the Hyde Park United Methodist Church on Wednesday, November 5.

The steering committee, in its ministry to the cycle clubs has the possibility of being under the supervision of the Young Adult Action of the UMC directed by Rod Barr of the Methodist Church Board of Missions. This group deals with experimental ministries and would like to involve itself in a direct contractual agreement with us. Mr. Slutz summarized his understanding of the purpose of our committee as follows:

1. **Provide counseling and understanding for what Skip is trying to do.**
2. **Be of help by knowing the right people and having contacts which will be readily available to the bikers when needed.**

Skip stated his apprehension and concern in dealing with these motorcycle clubs. He sees his role and concerns of his ministry as follows:

1. His being a servant. (Sometimes this means being used.)
2. How and when to reach out to them without turning them off.
3. Knowing just what the "Good News" might be to them.
4. Learning how to listen to them.

One suggestion was that maybe this should be a full-time ministry. Skip replied that if the gangs knew he was a full-time minister to them only that would turn them off.

A question was raised as to why and when do club members quit.

Skip answered:

1. Their marriage unravels, creates hassles for them, or their wives give them an ultimatum.
2. They get tired of being harassed and arrested.
3. Age, they just grow up.

What should be the immediate concern of this committee?

1. Create a sensitivity to this meaningful ministry within the church.
2. Continue talking to Rod Barr and his agency to obtain advice and ideas.

The following comments are from the minutes of the January 20, 1970 meeting by Bobbie Stinson, secretary:

The following are portions of the various statements made at our January 20 meeting and are by no means verbatim.

Faye Flint: *This ministry is so tough on people with gray hair because it is so different. However, it is so exciting in the ministry for people who are without the Good News. The people in the church need this ministry as well as the groups (gangs) we are dealing with.*

Jewel Smith: *Older people are very slow to change and they get in a rut. You can only go so far with them. However, the church is changing, and in ten year's time, how many people at the Northside UMC will be living. They have had the church all their lives, now they need to give the church, too.*

Brother Theodore: *Skip represents the church to these gangs. He represents Christ.*

Dr. Colaw: *One interesting insight that came to me is that what you [Skip] are doing is interesting and exciting, but I have been struggling to fit it into some category that*

relates to ministry. I don't think I can go where you go. This ministry relating to gangs is doing as much for the church as it is to the gangs.

Faye Flint: *They have experienced this rejection from the establishment.*

Jewel Smith: *Skip doesn't allow them to be rejected in the church.*

Leonard Slutz: *Is this a big enough work that it should be full-time? My own feeling is "no." Skip can do much more to bring about understanding as a minister of a church, as a minister of an inner-city church.*

Bill Garrett: *Are there specific things about this work that call for a group beyond us? What kind of things are needed by Skip?*

At this point, in the meeting, our committee discussed the minutes of our November 5, 1969, meeting and looked at additional ways our committee may be of help:

1. **Provide sociological and psychological help for some of the groups Skip works with.**
2. **Help find them jobs.**

Faye Flint stated that this is not just Skip's ministry, but the Cincinnati District's.

Rod Barr, from the New York office of Urban Young Adult Action of the United Methodist Church, pointed out that it is asking too much for the Northside UMC to carry such a ministry financially. This committee should look wider than Northside and even wider than United Methodists.

Dr. Colaw, Brother Theodore, and Faye Flint will be making contacts concerning funding.

Funding the ministry was going to be the most difficult task of the steering committee. Dr. Colaw, at the November 5th meeting, stated that conference funds were not available. He suggested we look to another committee within the district or conference to raise funds.

The committee decided that a letter should be sent to several selected persons in the Cincinnati area to enlist financial support for this ministry. (At the meeting, the budget reflected that the projected monthly expenses would be more than seven hundred dollars.) Dr. Colaw would write the letter and Faye Flynt stressed, "It would be helpful in the letter to mention the size of the sub-culture of the motor-cycle gangs. With over twenty gangs, the men and women involved would be close to one thousand.

"Another thing: something in the letter should emphasize the need for confidentiality. Skip's contacts would end quickly if the young men ever found out that 'citizens' such as those who would receive the letter were involved in this way. In the second place, Skip is playing a dangerous game. Murder is not unthinkable, and the use of drugs by the young men and their women friends is a very real aspect of the situation."

From the advice of the committee, Dr. Colaw wrote the following letter to a selected number of citizens in the Cincinnati area.

This letter is to provide you with an opportunity to participate in an exciting new kind of ministry. One of the concerns of the traditional church is our inability to reach persons who are in what is known as the "sub-cultures." Fortunately, a young minister here in Cincinnati has come up with an exciting approach to one of these groups. The Rev. Gene Skipworth is now conducting a ministry to motorcycle clubs. He has an interest in these young men and a unique ability to communicate with them and relate to them. He has been identified with several of the gangs (there are over 20 in Cincinnati), and has been accepted very genuinely by many of them, and has been able to receive a considerable number into the fellowship in the Christian Community.

A few of us here in the community have formed a sponsoring committee to help guide this creative new venture. We are, therefore, desperately in need of some funds, as there is no organization providing money at this time. Those of us whose names are listed below are engaged in the effort to raise approximately $2500 to provide him with money by which he can minister to these men.

Involved in this, of course, is the paying for the cycle which he now has which enables him to actually participate with them in some of their activities.

This project has the endorsement of the Young Adult Commission of the United Methodist Church and the approval of Bishop Roger Blanchard of the Episcopal Church of Cincinnati, and Monsignor Asplin of the Roman Catholic Diocese, and Dr. Howard Brown, superintendent of the United Methodist Church.

We are now venturing to ask a few of Cincinnati's leading citizens who have not only a sensitive social conscience but a vital concern for the missional life of the church to contribute from $25 to $50 to this greatly needed project. We think there can come out of this a model which might be pursued in other cities. We must do something to reach this part of our society which now feels alienated from all traditional forms such as the church. Incidentally, for the safety of Mr. Skipworth there is a need to not make any public announcement concerning this activity.

If you feel an inclination to participate in this phase send your gift in the enclosed envelope either to the Francisan Development Fund, 1615 Vine Street, c/o Ulme Kuhn, O.M.F. or the Methodist Union, 617 Vine Street, Provident Band Bldg., Cincinnati, Ohio.

I was already racing motocross and that was expensive, but it was a great tool for having an in with the outlaw biker clubs. They didn't want to race and they thought guys who did were crazy. They told me, "Hell, you got fifty bikes going full-throttle trying to be first at one little corner. You have to have brains in your asshole to do that. That's why they have all those ambulances at those races."

They judged a person from the neck down and racing impressed them. The committee felt it was important to fund the racing since it was such a great hook.

Jim Adams wrote in the *Cincinnati Post and Times Star* in November of 1971: "Skip's interest in motorcycles in general and racing in particular has endeared him to some of the toughest outlaw motorcycle gangs in the city."

Herschal Benkert and Bernie Evanshine also raced motorcycles and they were a great help in this aspect of my ministry. Herschal maintained my racing bike and he and Bernie helped coach me to be competitive. It was from Hercshal that I purchased my racing bikes as I continued to improve and develop my skills. I began with a 125cc Penton and a 250cc Huskavarna. I finished my racing career with a Maco 405cc from Jade Enterprises of Harrison, Ohio.

When I first began racing, I didn't notice outlaw type spectators. Once I became involved with them, more would show up and act as my cheering section. They would let everybody know they were there for the preacher.

When they would come to the entrance gate, they would try to get in free by saying, "We're the pit crew for the preacher."

If I broke down or crashed on the track, they would have people along the course to help me get back in the race. One time I got caught up in a mud hole and several came wading in through the mud to push me out and then yelled at me, "You better get your ass in gear and catch up."

The bike the UMC bought for me to use in the ministry.

After a race

Near the end of a race

Talking to the starter

Start of a race

Racing a Maico

Racing motorcross

They became very frustrated at my lack of winning. "What the hell, preacher, you got God on your side and you still can't win. Hell, nobody else prayed this morning and they're beatin' your ass off." When I did win a trophy, they would accuse me of cheating since I knew the "Man upstairs."

The most important fundraising issue was buying a bike to ride on the street with them that would meet the expectations and image of the bikers. The bike could not be, as they referred to it, a "Jap bike." When someone told them about the bike they owned and it wasn't a Harley, they got the question, "That's for the sidewalk, what do you ride on the street?" It should be a Harley and it had to be "chopped" and customized to look different from a stock bike off the showroom floor.

The bike could be a limy, a bike built in England, like a Triumph, Norton, or BSA. A limy would be acceptable but it had to have the front forks radically raked, the body chopped, no front fender, thin front wheel, ape-hanger handle bars (which were high risers), extended, lots of chrome, a customized tank, and a paint job. The committee found a good used Triumph Bonneville. They chose the Triumph because it was cheap and Marlon Brando rode one in the movie, *The Wild Ones*. The bike cost one thousand dollars.

A member of a United Methodist Church that Mr. Benkert knew owned a speed shop which customized cars and bikes. We explained to him what we needed and why. In three weeks, he had the bike ready. It had a beautiful customized paint job with many other features that made it readily acceptable and admired by all the bikers. The bikers said it looked cherry. The only flaw it had according to the president of the Iron

Horsemen was that it had "titty blue" handle grips. The customizing job cost $439.22 as recorded by our treasurer, Faye Flynt.

The fundraising came from several sources. One of the most important was speaking to churches and groups about my ministry. Faye Flynt and Bill made many of those contacts for me. One of the most exciting was an invitation from Emerson Colaw, later to become bishop of the United Methodist Church, to speak at the National Conference on Evangelism in New Orleans.

Many individuals and churches in our district and conference and other denominations were very helpful in providing funds. The Episcopal Diocese of Cincinnati, the Episcopal Bishop Blanchard, and the Franciscan Seminary on Colerain Avenue were regular contributors.

There were other expenses we didn't expect. When a biker was sick or hurt or lost his job, we helped with rent or mortgage payments, and purchased clothing and groceries for him and his family. I bought an alarm clock for one guy because he almost lost his job being late for work. We gave Bibles to those who wanted them. We gave going-away gifts to those who left for the service. We took care of some medical bills and prescription costs. We made small personal loans. Mrs. Flynt organized the fundraising, deposited the funds, and kept the records.

An important task of the steering committee was creating awareness in the churches of the subculture of the outlaw motorcycle clubs of the Cincinnati area. When Bishop Blanchard of the Episcopal Diocese of Cincinnati was approached about this ministry, he said, "I didn't know there were any motorcycle gangs in Cincinnati." The call to minister to the outlaw bikers of our community was difficult when the church didn't know they existed. The path of those I worked with and the path of the church seldom crossed.

Bikers made it more difficult by putting up a wall in that path. They distanced themselves and wanted to be separate from "citizens," as they called them. They put everyone in two categories, themselves and jags, sometimes referred to as stonejags. Jags were most citizens, especially college students, cops, politicians, preachers, church folk, and teachers. I was obviously in the jag category. Being a preacher, I was referred to early on as a stonejag. When I first met the BIA at the first dance, I felt the wall go up immediately. It took a long time before I was able to have conversations with them.

They may have held their heads up high and stood straight with their chest out and shoulders square, but, in a figurative sense, their heads were cast down. I saw in them despair, discouragement, and depression. They seemed lost, bewildered, and hopeless. Many of them viewed life with a chip on their shoulder. They were defensive and angry. For some, their attitudes were expressed in hate-talk. I heard them say many times, "Nobody gives a shit about us and that's what we think about them."

Big Dave, of the Iron Horsemen, told me about a lady who knocked on his door during a snow storm and asked him if he would come out and change a flat tire on her car near his driveway. "While I changed it for her she noticed my colors I had on over my leather jacket. Then she treated me like I was just scum. She didn't even thank me. The next time some old bitch comes around and wants me to help her, I'll tell her to get screwed. They just don't give a shit about people like us."

When I heard and experienced so much of their anger, discouragement, disregard for their own lives, and a hopeless sense for their future, I would mention the prophet Isaiah in my conversation with them. I would tell them that Isaiah had an almost impossible task of proclaiming hope and direction for the patriarchs and people of his time. I told them what he had to say about hope:

> Have you not known? Have you not heard?
> The Lord is the everlasting God, the Creator of the ends of the earth.
> He does not faint or grow weary; his understanding is unsearchable.
> He gives power to the faint, and strengthens the powerless.
> Even youths will faint and be weary, and the young will fall exhausted;
> but those who wait for the Lord shall renew their strength,
> they shall mount up with wings like eagles,
> they shall run and not be weary,
> they shall walk and not faint (Isa. 40:28–31 NRSV).

They needed to hear those words of hope and assurance. They needed to know that their lives could take on a new and positive direction.

Parents played a major role in the negative and hostile attitudes of the bikers I met. I heard very few stories of love, compassion, support, or encouragement given to these young men by a parent.

Many times I appeared in court with bikers. Too often I heard a mother or father say to the judge, "I don't give a damn what you do with him." I will never forget the look on Chief's face, a member of the BIA, when his mother said that to the judge.

He had been looking down at the floor. After she made her statement to the judge, Chief raised his head and just stared straight ahead. It was as if he was surprised and taken aback to hear it from his mother. Even though he had no reason to expect support and compassion from his mother, his face still registered shock at her words. On the outside, he tried to act like her comments didn't bother him. He even gave a weak chuckle as if to say, "That didn't hurt a bit." When his mother spoke those words, I felt a great deal of pain and hurt for him.

Deep down, Chief and all the young men who had a similar experience were aching for a touch from their mothers, a word of encouragement, an expression of love.

When I visited Chief at the County Workhouse, he told me about the many nights when he and his brothers would have to sleep on the front porch, even in cold weather, because one of his mother's boyfriends was in the house with her. He said whenever the front door was locked, they were to stay outside because that was the signal she had company.

He said when he was in high school, she was never home. Even after all she put him through and the way she treated him, he asked me to visit her in the hospital when she was very ill. At the hospital she told me, "You are leading my son down the road to hell. What are you trying to do with those young men?"

One night a drunken father came to the house to fight me because he said I caused his son to join the BIA. I didn't even know his son had a father. Bones never talked about having a father. I had often seen this man, who now stood at my door, at Knowlton's corner in Northside in front of White Castle. Whenever I saw him, he looked like the typical street drunk. Standing there on the porch of the parsonage, it sounded to me as if he had been dealing with guilt for a long time, as if he had no one, nothing. That no one cared. Now, coming to the house was his way of taking it out on someone. "Come out here where I can get a piece of you, you son of a bitch. I'll teach you a lesson."

I stepped out on the porch and asked him, "Why don't we walk down to Maria's and have a cup of coffee?"

He told me to go to hell. I offered him two dollars and told him to stop in at Maria's and have a drink on me. He stood there and looked at me, grabbed the money and walked toward Maria's.

Filthy Phil told me how he wished his father would have stayed home because there were so many things he would have liked to do with him.

As plans were being made for a wedding of one of the Iron Horsemen, the groom came to me and told me how disappointed he was that his mother would not come to his wedding. While he was in my study with his fiancé, his mother called and told me I had no business associating with the likes of him since I was a minister. She said, "Ever since he left home he has caused me nothing but grief. I'm surprised you can't see he is no good with that long hair and all his dirty friends." He actually wanted her to come to his wedding.

The saddest wedding I ever conducted involved a Henchman. It was going to be a small, friendly, informal, and happy wedding at the church. The groom, the bride, and her family had made big plans for a wonderful day. He had shaved, gotten a suit and haircut, and told the Henchmen, out of respect for the church, his bride, and her family, they were not to wear their colors. At the receiving line at the back of the church, I asked him where his folks were. He said his mother would not come to his wedding; and furthermore, she told him she wouldn't even come to his funeral.

Round said that in 1969, a tornado swept through Northern Cincinnati and several Horsemen attempted to help the police with traffic and the injured. He said, "Porky gave mouth-to-mouth to a lady who was severely injured and a cop came over and chased him away. Hell, Porky saved the bitch's life and what did he get for it? The goddamn cop told us to get the hell out of the area. It was our goddamn neighborhood! Porky and five other brothers live down the fuckin' street. That's the last time we are going to lift a finger to help anybody; screw 'em."

Responses like those from citizens only increased their feelings of anger, resentment, and defensiveness. They had no interest in anything or anyone outside their own. The walls were up. On Tuesday, January 19, 1971, I appeared on the Nick Clooney television talk show with Round. He was asked what he thought of me and my involvement with the Iron Horsemen. It was a big surprise to me when he said, "The preacher's OK, and the guys don't mind him being around. We dig him."

Getting a positive comment about me was unexpected. I had to be careful in knowing what to say, when to say it, and how to say it when I was with the bikers. Their negative concept of life left little room for giving accolades. They showed little warmth and compassion toward others. They were skeptical, distrustful, unfriendly, hostile, and, because of the wall they built up, hard to get to know. When persons were introduced to any of them, they seldom received a handshake or eye-to-eye contact. They were skeptical and trusted very few people outside their circle.

They rarely offered any kind of praise about a cop. Not too surprisingly, cops they did have good things to say about owned motorcycles. They got to know them at cycle shops, races, field meets, rallies, or, of course, their own run-ins with the police.

As some of the police found out about me and became acquainted with me, they either thought I was stupid for getting involved with bikers, or they wanted to help me by providing me information about some of the bikers who may be potential threats to me. The police officers who were helpful to me referred to the bikers as loose cannons. They were helpful by telling me about their own experiences with individual bikers and particular outlaw clubs. I had arranged for two of them to come to the house to talk to Hawk, president of the Satan's Angels, about a grievance the Angels had with the police. These police officers also felt there had to be a different kind of communication between the police and clubs besides the hard looks, night sticks, guns, and feelings of doing away with each other. A great deal of pressure was released when policemen were willing to talk it over with some bikers about a grievance.

But, none of the clubs, and very few individual bikers, had anything good to say about the police, especially the Brothers In Arms. The Fifth District, which covered Northside, always seemed to be in a battle with the BIA. The police had a right, in many cases, to be hard on the BIA. Roach called me one night and asked me to come down to the police station and help him get home. He had been beaten by a cop with a night stick and was a bloody mess. He was picked up near the church and taken in because he was suspected of breaking and entering. He resisted the cops and was beaten.

At one of the BIA meetings in the basement, they were discussing plans for a party. Everybody was hassling and arguing about where and when. They asked me what I thought about it and what I thought they should do.

"Why not forget the party and challenge District Five police to a touch football game?" I was always looking for some way to build a better relationship between the BIA and the police.

The guys all looked at me as if I had gone completely nuts.

"Man, you are really starting to act and talk like a preacher. What do you think we are, grade school kids?"

After Bones had his say, everyone got real quiet as if they were thinking about the possibilities and how it might play itself out.

Butch said, "Think about it. Just think about it. Be quiet and just think about it."

Sarge got up and walked across the room running his hands through his long blond hair. He looked at Filthy Phil and they both began to smile. The kind of smile a poker player might have when he knew he had a winning hand.

Sarge said it first and spoke for everyone, "Me across the line of scrimmage from Sergeant Ross." It was as if he was playing out a big fantasy in his mind.

Filthy Phil added, as visions of mayhem gleamed in his eyes, "And no holds barred, everything equal."

All of a sudden, everyone started speaking up about who they thought would win, or be able to walk off the field. Butch got everybody under control. "OK, preacher, you go talk to them and get it arranged. We will go anytime, anyplace, under any rules. And do it quick, we are ready to go."

At last I thought I had a start in building up a better relationship between the police and the BIA. It would turn out to be the first time anything positive had been done to get a better understanding underway with the police and the community. I went to the police station and talked to the officer in charge.

"I've been in contact quite a bit lately with the Brothers In Arms and I would like to suggest something to help you in your relationship to them. Right now they have some really hard feelings toward the police department. I see nothing but bad experiences for the two of you the way it stands now. They want to improve that relationship and I am sure you would like to see it improve also.

"One way that relationship can be improved came from a suggestion from them. They would like to challenge the Fifth District to a touch football game. This is an opportunity for them to meet you and get to know you in a different role. It would be a great chance for you to get to know them as individuals.

"They suggest that the game be advertised so the community of Northside can see their desire to foster a more positive image. It is also a chance for you to show that the police are interested in relating to and getting more personally involved in the community. You have nothing to lose and everything to gain."

He showed no expression while I was presenting him the idea so I didn't expect too much of a positive feedback.

"No, there is no way that we could let the men get involved in such a thing. I appreciate what you are trying to do, but it just isn't possible."

"But, the Brothers In Arms said they would be willing to play anyplace and anytime for the convenience of your men. They said you could even have your own men officiate. There wouldn't have to be more than five guys on each team if that would help."

I sensed the officer digging his heels into sand on the other side of the counter. I think he was losing his patience with me. I was only thinking what I would tell the guys.

"No," he said, "we just don't have insurance to cover such a thing."

When he started to walk away, I said, "They don't have any insurance of any kind."

He kept walking, and once inside his office, closed the door.

How were they going to react to this turndown? What would this do to my credibility with them? They already had nothing to say that was positive about the police and this rejection of a great idea would only add to their mistrust and feelings that the police had no interest in improving relations.

Of course, as time went on, there were more incidents of conflict between the BIA and the police. Several of the Brothers were arrested and sent to the state prisons in Lebanon and Ross for assault, breaking and entering, stealing and selling stolen property, domestic violence, counterfeiting, and drug dealing. Several, like Sarge, joined the military. Some, like Cherokee and Filthy Phil, dropped out of the club and left the area. A few quit riding and wearing the colors and went back to their families and jobs. In less than six months after my visit to the Fifth District, the Brothers In Arms no longer existed. I often wondered what might have been the result if the police had been willing to have a touch football game with the BIA.

There were other times I had to step in between the police and an outlaw club.

One of those times was when I had a biker wedding at the church. A police car patrolling the area saw all the bikes pulled up next to the church and called for assistance. During the wedding ceremony, the bride and groom were standing before me, repeating the vows. In the back of the sanctuary, six cops entered and interrupted the service. I stopped the service. I looked at them as they stood behind the back pews. Everyone turned to look at them.

I saw arrogance and intimidation from their stance and demeanor. They didn't take off their hats and didn't appear to show any respect for being in the sanctuary.

I paused for a moment and told them (I didn't ask), "Please take off your hats and be seated. Show some reverence and respect. You are in the House of God and you are interrupting a wedding ceremony."

They slowly walked out into the narthex and left.

Outlaw motorcycle clubs didn't have anything good to say about the militant left-wing radical groups who were constantly trying to enlist their help. The Weathermen of Cincinnati wanted the Iron Horsemen to give them some muscle and armed protection at a political demonstration they had planned in the city. They also wanted the Horsemen to help them destroy some government property. The Horsemen weren't flattered by the invitation. I asked them why they didn't help since the Horsemen shared the same feelings of antagonism toward the system that the SDS, Weathermen, Black Panthers, Hippies, and street freaks seemed to have. One of the Horsemen explained, "Those people are so screwed up. We wouldn't lift a finger to a twat of one of those long-haired bitches."

Later I read that the Hell's Angels of California had been asked to participate in a demonstration by providing security for a left-wing radical group. The Hell's Angels used it as an opportunity to "bust some heads." The groups with whom I thought the bikers would share something in common were not looked on with favor by the bikers.

Another way they had of putting up walls was called "warpin' a citizen out of his mind," "blowin' his mind," "freakin' him out," or "torkin' him out." A member of the Henchmen said, "We use the image to 'tork people out of their minds.' You should have seen us at the auto show. [Each year there is a big auto/motorcycle show where some of the outlaw clubs and American Motorcycle Clubs display their bikes.] There were twelve of us lined up French kissing each other. You should have seen the jags get messed up. Then we took one of our boots and each of us pissed in it and the guy at the end drank out of it. The jags got stone-torked out of their minds."

Such gross behavior was not always the case. Nevertheless, they still tried to mess with people's minds. One day a boy scout executive was visiting the church office and we were talking about the scout troop that meets in the church. Two Devil's Disciples came in and sat down in the office where we were talking. The scout leader was shocked into stone silence. From his expression, I was sure it was the first time he had come face-to-face with an outlaw biker. He didn't want to look too shocked or afraid, so he just smiled and we went on with our conversation. The bikers just listened.

I left the room to attend to something else and overheard them say to him, "Hey man, what do we look like to you?"

Again there was stone silence and he finally said, "Well, you look like you probably ride a motorcycle."

Their behavior was the biggest issue that built walls between them and others. Vic Frederickson, an Episcopal priest friend of mine and member of the steering committee, asked me to invite the Iron Horsemen to his ordination at Christ Church downtown. He wrote, "I would be happy to welcome any cycle group to this event. Their presence would help our congregation realize that we have a ministry to these men, especially financially on their part. Also, this is part of my ministry, so if anyone wants to come, bring them, colors and all, just as they are. You could park your cycles right behind the chapel in the alley, we own the property. Peace. Vic."

When the Horsemen entered the sanctuary for this very formal and significant service of ordination, they expected the people to react in shock as they were ushered to their seats. The usher took us to our pew as if we were regular worshippers. We sat about the middle of the sanctuary on the left side. After we were seated, an elderly lady sitting in front of us turned around and saw the Horsemen and asked, in a very pleasant way, "Good evening. Where are you from?"

Cutter stood up and turned around to show her the Iron Horsemen colors and said to her, "We are the Iron Horsemen from Cincinnati."

"Well, we are glad to have you."

Cutter was surprised at her comment and blurted out rather loudly, "You are?" Everyone in the several rows in front of the Horsemen turned around and looked very surprised to see twenty-one churlish-looking Iron Horsemen talking to a sweet little old lady.

At the reception following the service, a punch bowl was set up in a fountain-type arrangement and, instead of using the glasses provided, some of the Horsemen rummaged through the kitchen, brought out large glasses and made sure everyone was watching as they used the glasses to drink the punch.

It was not unusual to see club members urinating on the sidewalk in front of pedestrians. They would be loud and abusive to customers in stores. They wanted everyone to feel menaced. In one convenience store they tossed wine, beer, and soft drink bottles back and forth. When I was out in public with them I was always afraid I would be embarrassed by their behavior. If I was embarrassed, I apologized to the people being offended and told the guys to knock off what they were doing. Usually, I just left.

I often said, "Knock it off; we are all going to get thrown out of here. Worse yet, they will call the police." Most store and bar owners knew if they called the police on them, they would be back eventually to trash the place. Club members would always say something like, "Preacher, if you don't like it, get the hell out of here." They said they had an image to uphold.

At a bar in Cleves, a Satan's Angel stripped the clothes off his boozed up mama and threw her on her back on a pool table. He then took down his pants and climbed on top of her in front of everyone. I grabbed him by his boots and pulled him off the table. He took a pool stick, broke it against the side of the pool table, and with a broken half in his hand, said, "OK, preacher, where is your fuckin' hose?"

Lucky for me, the owner had called the police when the Satan's Angels first arrived at the bar. The cops took him away in cuffs. To the Satan's Angels, the bar owner and I were the bad guys. They threw a chair through a window and they told me to mind my own business. Then they left. And, I had forgotten my hose.

I was with the Iron Horsemen when they attended the movie *Easy Rider* at a Hyde Park theater. They sat in the middle of the theater and took up two rows of seats. They arrived early and made a grand entrance as if to say, "Take a good look, this movie is all about us." Most of them carried in jugs of Mogan David wine.

The movie was about two cyclists trying to do their own thing. They were long-haired, bearded hippie motorcyclists, perfect symbols of rebellion against middle-class conformity. Their names were Billie and Wyatt, names that reflected outlaws of the past when beards, long-hair, and individualism were accepted.

Toward the end of their journey one admits "We blew it." They found their odyssey of sharing time at a commune, drugs, booze, and all the undisciplined behavior of the open road was not the way to express individualism. They discovered that their appearance disgusted and annoyed people. After they tried to get a meal at a diner in a small redneck town, they left when they were not served. As they stopped that evening to bed down at their campfire, some local good ol' boys beat them while they were sleeping. One of them, a hitchhiker they picked up, played by Jack Nicolson, was killed. The movie ends with the two bikers being gunned down by shotgun blasts from a couple of citizens in a pick-up truck.

During the movie the Horsemen would make loud comments like, "Yeah man," "Fuckin' right, man." If the dialogue was something they would say or represented what they stood for, one of them would turn around to the audience and yell, "Anybody got a problem with that?" Everyone in the theater knew who the Iron Horsemen were. No one challenged them. No one said a word in response to their comments or behavior.

At the dramatic and tragic ending of the movie, the Horsemen were the first ones to stand to leave. They turned around and looked at everyone and Round said, "Nobody leaves 'til we do." Farmer John and Crazy Horse stood at the end of each aisle with their hands folded in front of them like they were the groomsmen at a wedding. When the last Horseman left the aisle, then Farmer John and Crazy Horse followed. I was seated in the middle of the first row of Horsemen and one of the last to leave. I walked out in front of Farmer John. As we were walking up the aisle, he said, "We should have taken an offering, Preacher."

Easy Rider really enhanced their image. The theme of the movie of a biker's independence, being one's self, doing one's own thing, being your own man fit the role and image they were after.

When the Horsemen appeared with me on the Nick Clooney television talk show, one of the sponsors was Kentucky Fried Chicken. They devoured the samples in a way that embarrassed me, the host, stage crew, and the audience. Round appeared on stage with a drumstick in his pocket. It was all a part of playing the role.

The problem with the image game was that the citizens reacted the way the bikers expected them to—shocked. I experienced this reaction of the citizens one night when I pulled in on my bike at a Frisch's drive-in wearing the colors of the Brothers In Arms. When I stopped and shut off the engine, the people in the cars on each side of me locked their doors and rolled up their windows. Such reactions only fed the role played by the biker. When a person did not show signs of surprise or disgust, that only pushed the biker to try harder. When the scout executive did not get freaked out, the Disciples were surprised and disappointed. He left before they tried anything else.

Every time bikers wore their colors in a public place, they expected people to react with fear. They always wore a game face. The meaner and harder look they could put on their face, the better. They were more concerned about scaring hell out of people and looking like hardcore cycle-trash than anything else. They would sometimes try to intimidate people with their loudness and rudeness. If anyone stared at them, and most did, they would be confrontational by saying, "What you lookin' at, jag?" If someone gave them a hard look as if to say, "You don't scare me," they would hover over them and stare that person down. So many times I had to step in and say, "Let's go sit down."

I know what they would do today if they saw a loud inconsiderate guy talking on his cell phone in a restaurant. One of them would walk over, lean into his face

and tell him, "Get off that phone or I will shove it down your throat." Since the cell phone can be such an inconsiderate and rude intrusion today, I wish a Filthy Phil, or Farmer John, or Crazy Horse could be with me to get some loud-mouth off his phone. I don't have the spine.

Crazy Horse never liked the idea of people thinking the Horsemen were violent. He said, "It all depends on where you are and what the situation is. Normally, the Horsemen as a club are peaceful people when they are by themselves; but the trouble starts when they go somewhere where citizens are and the citizens can't get along with Horsemen.

"There is so much we will take, and I don't care who is in the way, when it gets started, somebody is going to get their brains beat out. You just can't take anymore. There will be some wino or egghead who would come around and start a hassle. He thinks the wine or whiskey he was drinking could beat you up and make him look good in front of his friends.

"Well, it doesn't work that way. You got a family here as far as the Iron Horsemen go and I don't care if there are ten people who jump on one Horseman, or one guy jumps on a Horseman. When a guy jumps on a Horseman, he'd better have his stuff together because everybody will lunch him. It is all for one and one for all and when it is over you don't even think anything about it. Ninety percent of the time it is not the Horseman who caused the trouble; it is just that they run into people who want to hassle them all the time. We just don't like to be pushed around."

It was very difficult for anyone to get past their gross behavior to make any gesture of care and compassion. It was always a real test to the members of my church to see some of them come to worship with swastikas sewn to their colors, obscene words tattooed on their arms, and the four-letter word embroidered on their colors. They had to be reminded to leave their colors on the coat rack. Soon, they began to leave their colors on their bikes.

They were into building walls and setting themselves apart from others. I wanted to help them tear down those walls and replace them with a new open relationship with others based on the love of Christ in which they would genuinely care for others. I wanted them to feel acceptance in the shepherding care of God. They had little tolerance for those whose lifestyles, interests, and values were different than theirs. I wanted to sow the seeds of tolerance and acceptance. They lived by the code of "an eye for an eye." I wanted them to be touched and moved by the grace and love of Christ's power so that they would "not resist evildoers, but if anyone strikes you on the right cheek, turn the other also."

They were unwilling to trust others. I wanted them to see the good in people and trust them. I prayed that they would give Christ's grace a fresh new look to replace all the misconceptions and distortions they had of what and who He is and could be in their lives. Above all else, I wanted to do all I could, take all the risks, and provide all the time needed to enable Christ to make a difference in their lives.

CHAPTER SIX

Their colors were the most important feature that symbolized who they were. Their colors signified respect, power, and authority. Their colors drew immediate attention. When a member of one of the weaker clubs saw the colors of the Iron Horsemen, he was mesmerized as if he had seen his idol. Every club wanted their colors to get the same respect that was given the Brothers In Arms, Cobras, Iron Horsemen, Henchmen, or Outlaws. Seeing a biker in public wearing his colors was like seeing a peacock strut his stuff. Their colors represented manliness. For many, their colors represented all they were. They wanted people to see their colors and say, "There's a mean bastard, don't mess with him."

I first learned about the value of their colors from the Brothers In Arms. While they were in the basement of the parsonage, I overheard their conversation as they were preparing for a fight with the Fugeros who had ripped off two sets of colors of the BIA.

When I came down the stairs, they got quiet. I asked them, "Why are you guys going to pull a stupid stunt like this? Think. Beating someone with a chain belt is brutal. It's a crime."

Butch said, "Preacher, if we don't go after our colors, the Brothers In Arms will be nothing in this town." According to their criteria and standard for respect and honor, they were right. But, they were wrong.

I told them if they went through with the nonsense of a fight, I would call the police and there would no longer be a motorcycle club called the Brothers In Arms. Instead, I suggested that Butch meet with the leader of the Fugueros and retrieve their colors. I said I would go with him for the meeting.

The Fugueros were a Middletown-Dayton area outlaw club. Butch asked me, sarcastically, "What the hell would I tell him? We got this preacher, we meet in his basement, and he wants us to get together to talk about getting our colors back. Would that be all right with you?"

I told him how Ivan, one of the officers of the Outlaws, described the Fugueros. Ivan said, "They are not serious about what they are doing. It's a game. A phase of life they are going through. We don't have wives and children around us. With the Outlaws, it's a 100 percent way of life. It's not something you say but what you live."

I went on to say, "If Ivan is right, and that is the way the Fugueros really are, they would welcome a call from you to talk it over. I am sure they don't want a war over having two sets of your colors. Make the call to the president and tell him to meet us by himself at the Broken Drum. And, tell him to bring the colors."

Butch called the president of the Fugueros and talked to his wife. His wife said he had been trying to call, that he wanted to get together with him.

They made the connection and they met without me or anybody else at a Gold Star Chili at Tri County. Butch came home with their colors.

When a gang's colors got messed with, they felt personally messed with. When their colors were not respected, they were not respected. The Henchmen went to war with the Cobras when a Cobra sewed the colors of one of the Henchmen on the seat of his pants. A member of the Gladiators made the mistake of stealing the colors of an Outlaw from his car. He made the bigger mistake of wearing them. The Outlaws found him while he was waiting at the bus stop on his way to work and whipped him with their chain belts. One of the most common reasons for a club fight was the theft of one club's colors by another club.

As a super-patriot protects and defends the flag, even more so the club member protected and defended his colors. There is a bit of irony in all this because the dirtier and more worn their colors were, the more that symbolized respect and devotion to them. I've seen bikers pour beer or oil, dump feces, and even urinate on their colors and then stomp in it with their boots. I've seen them rub dirt in them to make them look dirty and worn. They slept in them, worked in them, and cleaned the engines and bikes with them to add an extra bit of wear and tear. No biker wanted to have clean colors. Worn and dirty colors indicated that one had experience as a biker. It was proof of devotion and commitment just like a worn and frayed Bible indicates devotion and commitment of the Christian.

Their bikes were the other defining hallmark of who they were. Their bikes were always a topic of conversation when they got together. They devoted a lot of time, attention, and money on their bikes. The bike had to exhibit a lot of work and creativity and it never looked like it came straight from the showroom of a cycle shop. Their bike was always a used bike and the older the better. The more parts it had from older bikes, the more it was valued.

Japanese bikes were never accepted with the image and role of outlaw bikers. Some new upstart wannabe clubs, who were just into playing the role, started off with Hondas, Suzukis, or maybe Harley Sprints. To genuinely get into the role of the outlaw biker, the bike had to look the part and a chopped Harley was a must. A chopped Harley was stripped of the front fender, the back fender was cut smaller than stock, the front end was extended, it had lots of chrome and a customized paint job. Sometimes, a chopper looked like it had never seen paint. Some guys liked the raw black and no frills effect.

Honda motorcycles had an ad that said, "You meet the nicest people on a Honda." The bikers I rode with did not think that was the case with a Harley. "We ride a Harley and we are not the nicest people you would ever meet."

When a club parked their Harley Davidsons, there was an unwritten rule that only Harley Davidsons parked near them. At an Iron Horsemen wedding in Ault Park, the Iron Horsemen had their bikes parked in a line in front of the garden house where I conducted the wedding. Two guys on Hondas parked beside them. When the Horsemen came back to their bikes they were surprised to see the Hondas and the two riders sitting there.

Crazy Ron approached the two Honda riders and asked them, "Why are you parking those two piles of shit next to our Harleys?" The two Honda riders were still sitting on their bikes taking in all the activity of the wedding as Horsemen gathered around the cake and kegs of beer. Crazy Ron walked up to them. Other Horsemen began to gather around Crazy Ron and the two Honda riders to take in the conversation. Richie began to take the caps off the gas tanks of the two Hondas. The Horsemen gathered in closer.

Another Horseman asked, "Didn't you hear what the Brother asked? What the fuck are you doing sitting here on those Japs with our Harleys?" Crazy Ron took some wedding cake and slowly and deliberately stuffed it into the gas tanks of the Hondas. As he did he looked straight into the eyes of the two unsuspecting men. The two Honda riders were shocked and scared as they sat on their bikes with their mouths wide open. Crazy Ron said, "Don't ever park those pieces of shit near a Horsemen's bike again."

Their bikes were often kept in the kitchens and living rooms of their homes during the winter or when repairs had to be made. A Devil's Disciple's son used the heads off his Harley's engine for a play table while he was customizing the front end.

The more I learned about this subculture of outlaw bikers, the more they learned about me. Racing motorcycles and having a street bike that they admired were two very important ways for me to get acquainted with them. Our mutual interest in bikes provided a genuine opportunity to build a relationship. They helped me when I needed repairs and they always came up with parts when I needed them. We traded parts and accessories, I helped tow them when they got stranded on the road, they borrowed my bike when their bike was down, and we often rode together.

They knew I was a preacher but they thought I was odd since I didn't fit their image of a minister. Demon, the president of the Satan's Sinners asked me when the topic of preachers came up, "How come preachers are so self-righteous? My mom's preacher comes to the house and everybody wants to hide. He's into hellfire all the time. Everybody is going to hell but him. The last time I saw him at my mom's house, he pointed his finger at me and told me I was lost. He got down on his knees and started praying real loud and crazy-like. Mom just sat there and I got the hell out."

One day two Iron Horsemen and their wives came to our home to visit. They were talking about a minister they had met a few days earlier. "Man, he was all jagged out to save our souls. There was no way he could hide what he was after. We flat out found what he was up to."

I thought to myself, *Skipworth, have you been so wishy-washy that they don't know that is what you are after?*

I said to them, "Well, what is so strange about that? What do you think I want to have happen? What do you think I am after? I want to get involved in your lives. I want to offer you the opportunity through Christ and the church to become your best selves."

"Yeah, but you're different, preacher."

I didn't know if that was a compliment or not. Maybe I was too wishy-washy. It might be that all I was after was to get them to accept me and not my message. Had I become a chameleon? Had I been offering them pablum?

I always tried to convey to my congregations, individuals, and especially the bikers the unique contribution, the abiding essence, or holy gift that God can give us. That unique gift is support, encouragement, and above all, for the bikers, affirmation that they were special.

One of the wives said, "You don't call us cycle-trash. You don't make us feel we are no good. You trust us, you open your house to us. You introduce us to your church people and don't make us feel ashamed. Barb Lambing and Jewel Smith invited us to their homes. That's what is so different."

A few of the bikers said they were glad we could talk about religion because I didn't make them feel condemned, stupid, or hopeless.

When Filthy Phil referred to me as "brother," it was in a religious sense. One could tell he capitalized Brother when he referred to me that way. "Me and Brother Skip have an appointment."

When they disagreed with me, which was often, they let me know. Our arguments were somewhat heated and sometimes in-your-face confrontational, which guaranteed they were alive and interesting. They knew that in our disagreements and arguments I would always tell them what I believed. They also knew I would never belittle them, their ideas or beliefs, or judge them as lost heathens. They trusted me. They were open with me. They understood there were certain things they could not and should not expect of me.

During one of those conversations, a Henchman asked me, "Can you be a Christian and still wear the colors of the Henchmen?"

My immediate reaction was to tell those who were there that they would have to change their lifestyles. I only saw the pot smoke floating in the air, their grim and haggard looks, their dirty clothes, a hand with a beer bottle or wine bottle in it, chains hanging off their jeans, guns in their boots, knifes in a leather sleeve, and their gods parked out front. I was not thinking about the words of Jesus when he talked about looking at the inside and not the outside. I was really caught up in the outside.

As I took time to think over my answer, I could see smiles on their faces and a kind of "we got him this time" as they passed around a jug of Mogan David wine. I told him, and I was looking at all of them, "It would be impossible to be a Christian if your colors took first place in your life before Christ. Your priorities have to be completely changed. He does not care what you look like or that you ride a bike or that your bike is really important to you. That's okay with him. All Christ wants is for you to love God as much as you love yourself. He wants you to love your neighbor as much as you love yourself. It's all about love. His kind of love which is doing for others, giving to others, thinking of others. Unselfish love. Can you do that? If you can, I want to talk to you. Think about it. You know where I can be reached. We can talk about it anytime, anyplace."

"That's goin' to be tough to do, preacher."

In the beginning, bikers would invite me to their parties just to see if I would show up. They weren't used to having a minister associate with them in the first place, let alone ride his bike across town to be with them at some dumpy bar. Soon, they expected me to join them and took it for granted that I would be there. In many cases, when they wanted to spend some time at a bar without having a hassle, they would say, "Preacher, we are going to meet at the Broken Drum. Wear your collar."

Once, a couple of local macho-studs at a bar challenged Cutter and Toad to a fight. Cutter and Toad told the bartender and the other people there, "Look, we didn't come here to cause trouble. We even brought our preacher with us. We just want to shoot some pool, have a beer, and listen to the music. Tell those jags to back off and there'll be no trouble. Did they bring their preacher?"

I guess it could be said they used me, but this unique relationship enabled me to help them in many ways as pastor and friend. It enabled me to spend time with them and be a minister to them. One could also say that my role with the bikers was not too much different from my role as pastor to the members of the Northside United Methodist Church. I wanted them to know that I was available to them and would take time for them whenever they needed me. It was important to them that someone would take time for them because it meant that someone cared.

I did pre-marital counseling and family counseling. I counseled mothers who were confused and upset that their sons were involved with outlaw biker clubs. When I visited the bikers in jails and hospitals, I had prayer with them and each time it was a great opportunity to offer the hopeful and life-building words of Christ. When I officiated at weddings and funerals, I always had a captive audience to whom I could preach and share the love of God in Christ. When I appeared in court with them, visited members of their families, and even heard their confessions, it was another chance for me to let them know Who I represented and why I was there.

Hearing their confessions was an unbelievable experience for me. I wasn't prepared for some of the things they shared with me. Some of their confessions revealed a hidden side of them that I didn't know existed. After hearing some of their confessions, I began to keep a catalogue of my own shocking responses in my mind: *I don't believe this. How could any human being do this? You got to be kidding. This is sick. He got away with this? Am I the only one he has told this to? Why is he telling me this? What can I do for him? What can I do for the victim?*

Some of the less horrible were not surprising: drugs; booze and what they did as a result; abusing their mama, girlfriend, or wife; stealing. Red, a member of the Cobras, told me that he went on a wild drunken rage and busted up his wife's prize possession, her flute.

One of the Horsemen confessed to me that he had just badly beaten a girl. It was late when he called and came over to the parsonage to see me the night of the beating. After he beat her, he rode around wondering what he should do. He was scared that he beat her too severely and came to see me because he thought he might have killed her. "Preacher, I just beat up a girl and I don't know if she is dead or not. She was just lying there and not moving. I want you to help me make a deal with God. If you hear my confession and if the girl lives, I promise I will go to mass again. Work it out for me."

Then he abruptly left my study. I went where he told me the beating took place. It was one of the bars where the Horsemen hung out. When I got there, I was told she was OK, but was taken to the hospital. When I got to the emergency room, her mother and boyfriend were with her.

I introduced myself to them and told them that the guy who beat her came to tell me about it and how sorry he was.

The mother was in tears, angry, and in shock to see her daughter look like she did. The mother said, "I don't care how sorry he is, he is going to pay." The boyfriend was also angry. He was at the bar and saw her get beaten. He stepped in to stop the Horseman, but when he did the other Horsemen who were there beat him and told him to stay out of it.

I went down to the nurses station and called the Horseman who did it and told him to meet me at the ER of the hospital. I told him, "If you don't meet me here and apologize to the girl and her mother and boyfriend, you will be in jail. In fact, I don't even know if an apology to them will keep you out of jail. And, it doesn't matter if you do or don't go to mass."

He met me at the ER and we went in together to see the girl, her mother, and boyfriend. Unbelievably, everybody acted civil. He sincerely apologized to the girl and especially, the mother. He shook hands with the boyfriend. He tried to explain that he had too much beer and it just got out of hand.

As we left the hospital together, I asked him if he had kept his promise and went to mass. He said, "I went but couldn't get in, damn it, because the church was locked. But, I kept my part of the deal."

He was one of the Horsemen who eventually ended up in the federal prison in Terre Haute, Indiana.

A bizarre confession came from Shadow, a Midnight Drifter, so named because he was so big he cast a big shadow. Shadow was one biker I thought would never darken my door to make a confession, or even come in to say hello. He looked like some mountain man who seldom came in out of the woods. He reminded me of Simon Kenton from the outdoor drama *Tecumseh*. He smelled like he had been in the woods for a long time. He was probably the strongest of any of the bikers I met. He could lift a Harley off the street and put it on the sidewalk with ease. He had a horribly threatening look in his eyes, which emerged from his thick bushy beard and long hair.

He told me, "I was stopped at a traffic light. I didn't see it change right away and the guy behind me honked his horn at me. It pissed me off so I turned off my engine, walked back to his car, and kicked in his side door. I walked away to go back to my bike and it hit me; he looked just like my grandpa who is dead. His wife was old, too. I got on my bike and just sat there. People all over the intersection looked at me like I was some animal. The old guy didn't do a thing. He must have been too afraid. I fired up my bike and left. I don't know what he did or where he is. I did a dumb thing, preacher. I am really sorry. I got to do something about it. The poor old man's door is busted up bad. And I scared the shit out of both of them. What can I do?"

"Let's go down to the police department in the area of the city where it happened. They may have a complaint filed. If they do, we will go from there. Can you pay for it?"

"I will do anything to make it right."

I couldn't believe it! This guy was really sincere. He wanted to make it right.

The older couple did file charges and Shadow not only paid the fine, but paid for the repair of the car door. After the appearance in court, he visited with the couple and continued his expression of remorse. He must have had a close relationship with his grandpa.

Wes, a member of the Stallions, called and told me that Simmons had been shot in the stomach playing around in their clubhouse with another brother. He asked if I would go to the hospital to see him. He said, "I think it is really bad, preacher." When I walked to his bed in the ER, Wes, Slim, and another Stallion were also there. Slim was a short baby-faced guy. He tried his best to look mean and fierce. Slim said, "Some of the other brothers are on the way."

He started on the usual nonsense that upstart biker clubs dole out. "Our brothers come first. We don't leave them behind."

I told him and Wes, "I didn't come here to hear how great the Stallions are. Did you elect a president yet?" It is a put-down to ask an outlaw biker club that didn't have a president if they had one. It means that no one in the club has the guts, strength, or savvy to be one. A club without a president tells a great deal about their strength and togetherness as a club. A club without a president is like a bunch of builders without a boss, or a church without a pastor.

After the nurse left, I moved over to the side of the bed. Simmons said, "Yeah, I know preacher, it was a stupid stunt we were doing. So, save it."

"You think I came here to tell you that? I have more important business with you. I know you are not stupid. I am here because you are smart, too smart to be a member of the Stallions." Wes and Slim both overheard me.

"I want to talk to you about going back to school. I know you only have a year and a half to finish. I want to come to pick you up when you get released from the hospital and take you home. Then, I want to stop over at your house while you are recovering and visit. I want to get to know you better. You have all kinds of possibilities ahead of you. Is that okay with you?"

Before he could answer, two more Stallions came and stood behind Wes and Slim. He immediately turned his attention to them.

I said hello to the other Stallions and was getting ready to leave. I asked Simmons if it would be okay for me to offer a prayer before I left. He looked at the others for a few seconds and said, "I don't think so, preacher."

As I walked out the door, I heard Slim say, under his breath, "Nice try, preacher."

It is ironic that after this encounter with the Stallions, I never saw them again or heard of them being anywhere where bikers gathered. The Stallions, like other wannabes, just dropped from the scene.

Willie told his dad to call me to come to see him at the hospital. He was in a serious bike accident and had a badly broken right leg. The doctors told him he may lose the leg. Being completely devoted to riding a bike and to a bike club like the Iron Horsemen, and to be told he may lose his kicking foot (for the kick starter) or his shifting foot (for the shifting lever) or the brake foot (for the brake lever) was critical to him.

When I saw him a couple of days after the accident, he was still heavily sedated from medication, but very upset and emotional. I had never seen an outlaw biker cry.

Gang wedding at the NUMC

Groom arrives for the wedding

Iron horseman gather after a wedding at the NUMC

Wedding processional

Gang wedding at the NUMC

A Horseman arrives for the wedding at the NUMC

His dad, who was with him when the ambulance brought him to the hospital and who was with him each time I visited, said, "The first thing he said was to call you. This is a very terrible thing to happen, but maybe it will get him to straighten up and get out of that gang. I know you are the only contact he has outside that bunch."

I spent about an hour with him that night. I held his hand and told him that not only would I pray for him then, but that I would make sure the people of the church had him in their prayers. I prayed with him and before he drifted off to sleep, I quoted the assuring words of Paul, "All things work for the good to them that love the Lord." I went on to try to be encouraging to him. "Willie, things will work out.

You may have never felt it before, but now, more than ever, God holds you in his hands. I will see you tomorrow."

I spent each day of that week with Willie in the hospital. He did not have to have his leg amputated. His leg improved with surgery and rehab and he was able to get back on his feet. I felt he genuinely enjoyed and felt encouraged by my visits. When I visited him and other Horsemen who were there in his room, they made way for me to be sure I was next to Willie.

With his steady improvement, there was always a warm welcome to me each time I came to visit. He seemed to be sincere when I asked if he would like for me to pray at the end of each of my visits. When other Horsemen were visiting him, I asked if we might have prayer together. It must have been an unbelievable picture seeing all of us around Willie's bed, holding hands in prayer; a minister in a blue suit and clerical collar, monstrous cycle-trash men with beards, long hair, dirty jeans, vulgar and worn colors, with chains hanging from their belts. Nurses seldom interrupted such a scene.

Willie went home to recover. It took a long time to recover completely. He was not able to ride his Harley for a long time. By the time he could, he had lost interest in the Horsemen. I married him and his girlfriend and they moved to Harrison Township where she taught school and he went back to his old job. He left the Iron Horsemen with a "medical retirement/disability." I never did think he was Horsemen material because when his girlfriend would go on occasional rides with the IH, she never wore colors. Willie was well-liked by his brothers. They always teased him about his girlfriend, "Willie, you got no control over your woman."

When I had weddings at the church, all the bikers knew that was another place that was the domain of the preacher. They knew it was my "turf" and that I would be doing "my thing" as they called it. I told them, "This is going to be a Christian wedding service and we will go by my guidelines and not yours."

In every phase of serving as pastor to them, they had to understand what I stood for and what the guidelines were. Setting up the guidelines early on always made my job as pastor to them less complicated and less difficult.

At weddings and funerals, if I did not share the Word with them, I would lose too much. I could not just be a friend to them or some weirdo preacher who liked to ride and race motorcycles. I would rather have been guilty of being too overbearing than too wishy-washy. I am sure I failed many times to proclaim the Word. Too often I was afraid. I tried too hard to say the right things, in the right way, and at the right time. I was too careful in trying to find the right opportunity to speak out. In doing so, I lost many opportunities. I had too many questions and not enough answers. But, at funerals and weddings, I made sure I proclaimed His love.

I had a short sermon for each of the funerals and weddings. In the sermon I told about the colors I wore, what they meant, and what they could do for a person's life. In one funeral of the Outlaws, where all the Outlaws from all over the country had gathered, I spoke about "Who We Go to to Get Our Lives Fixed." They asked me to "say a few words." They told me, "Don't make him

IRON HORSEMEN SHOVELING DIRT INTO GRAVE   Photographer: MELVIN GEIER

Horseman Funeral

or us out as boy scouts, but don't bad mouth us either." There were more than three hundred Outlaws from all over the country. The few words I spoke were:

We take a great deal of pride in our motorcycles. When they break down, we don't just let any Tom, Dick, or Harry work on them. Either we do it ourselves or we take it to the guy who we trust to get it running right again. We don't take a Harley to a Yamaha shop to get fixed; we take it to a Harley dealer. We want the right person to fix it for us. We want the person who made it to put it back together again. I race a Maico and if I can't fix it, I take it to the Maico dealer. If I take it to the right person, I know it will be fixed right. When we have things go wrong with our lives and we don't feel the joy of life that God intended for us to feel, then we should go to the One that made us. If we feel our lives are being wasted, we need to go to the One who can make it all right for us. If we feel nobody cares, we need to go to the One who loved us so much he gave His only Son. It is that love that sustains us and makes us all we were intended to be. Listen to this . . . apart from His Love, we never function like a perfectly tuned engine. So to be the man He wants each of us to be, we should let Him take our lives and fix them, make them right.

Iron Horseman leader buried

About 300 members of the "Iron Horsemen" and numerous other motorcycle clubs from all over the United States formed a funeral cortege Wednesday afternoon from the Anderson Funeral Home, Winton Road, Springfield Township, to Arlington Memorial Gardens to bury Ronald Lee Shelton, 29, president of the Kentucky chapter of the Iron Horsemen and national vice-president of the group. Shelton died at his home in Madisonville Sunday, police said. Shelton was buried in his Ironhorsemen's colors. At the grave site club members put mementoes such as different club patches. A collection was taken for the Rev. Gene Skipworth, Forest Chapel Methodist Church, Forest Park, who gave the eulogy. Rev. Skipworth presented the money to Shelton's widow. As a final salute, hand guns were drawn and fired into the air and the ground. Journal-News Photo by Mary Arthur.

Local paper covered the Horseman funeral

Mr. Ed Putman, a good friend of mine, and director of Anderson Funeral Home in a suburb of Cincinnati, handled one of the funerals I had with the Iron Horsemen.

I called him at his home one Sunday morning before church. I asked him if he would handle a funeral for me. He said yes, he would. I told him, "But the deceased in known as The Boss, a member of the Iron Horsemen. Will you still do the service?"

He assured me he would. He asked me to meet with him and some of the Iron Horsemen at his office on Monday morning to make the plans.

Ed, his wife, and children were long-time members of the Forest Chapel United Methodist Church. He was aware of the ministry I had with the bikers while I was pastor of the Northside UMC.

Ed went on to describe what took place then.

"Monday morning arrived and I wondered what I had gotten myself and the funeral home into. Skip led the group in and introduced everyone to me: Cathy,

The Boss's wife, Farmer John, Crazy Horse, and Round, the huge and intimidating president of the Iron Horsemen. I gathered the vital statistics that I needed—the death certificate, notices from the papers and other records. Mr. Shelton, The Boss, worked at the General Motors plant in Norwood, Ohio. I felt the ability to pay with the insurance was assured. The arrangements were made for a visitation on Wednesday afternoon and evening with the funeral service on Thursday morning."

Farmer John brought the clothing which was to be put on The Boss, consisting of Jeans and the Horsemen colors. The turnout for visitation was huge. Everyone wore their colors, even the children. One of the

Horseman's widow

Horsemen came to the door and asked Mr. Putman where he could change his clothes. He had on a good-looking suit and tie and wanted to change into his colors. He was a buyer of men's furnishings for Shillito's Department Store in downtown Cincinnati.

As the visitation was coming to an end, the brother of The Boss asked to spend some time with his brother as they were not on good terms at the time of the death. Ed and I went in the parlor with him to try to console the young man. As we stood there, we heard: pop, pop, pop. Ed asked, "Who would be setting off firecrackers at a time like this?"

The Boss's brother said, "Firecrackers, hell, those are gun shots!"

Just then, some guys were trying to get in the front door. Thank goodness, they were Horsemen who were outside waiting for The Boss's brother to leave.

They yelled, "Someone is shooting at us and our cars." One of the Horsemen grabbed the phone and made some calls. After he finished, he said, "We are going to war tonight!"

Ed called the township police and was told they would be patrolling all evening and be out in full force in the morning. Ed gave a sigh of relief after his call to the police and said, "I feel better but I still have to walk out to my car in the back of our parking lot." He put on his hat and coat, left all the outdoor and indoor lights on, and set off for his car. He said to me, as we were leaving together, "Who would shoot the preacher and funeral director?"

The morning arrived and it was a beautiful, sunny, and warm January day. The Putmans were married twenty-three years ago that day. He said, "I sure hope I get to keep our dinner reservations."

As people arrived for the 1:30 funeral service, they were from all over the three-state area—Ohio, Indiana, and Kentucky. They represented all the several chapters of the Iron Horsemen as well as several different outlaw clubs in the three states. When I came in, Ed told me he was not going to put up chairs in the parlor; there were too many people there. He said we would just stand shoulder to shoulder. That worked just fine.

As I started the service, the hubbub of 250–300 people quieted down and one could hear a pin drop. After the opening prayer, I asked everyone to repeat the Lord's Prayer. As soon as I said that, Ed told me later, "I stepped into the doorway of the parlor to back you up in your leading everyone in the Lord's Prayer. To my surprise, the room echoed with prayer. I thought, *Skip is really making some headway with these guys in his ministry to them.*"

After the final prayer, Ed asked everyone to pay their last respects to The Boss and then step outside to prepare to go to Arlington Cemetery in Mt. Healthy, which was about three miles away. As they filed past the casket, each of the bikers, the old ladies, the mamas, and the kids placed an emblem or pin from their own colors on the chest of The Boss.

As we prepared to leave for the cemetery, a plainclothes police officer was going to ride with me and Ed in the lead car, and another officer in plainclothes in the hearse.

Not everyone was going to the cemetery, but we had more than one hundred bikes and more than forty cars in the procession to the cemetery according to a reporter of the *Cincinnati Enquirer*. One could hear us leaving the funeral home and as we moved along the streets, people lined the streets on both sides to see the spectacle.

The newspapers really wrote up the funeral and the "parade atmosphere" of the procession. Crazy Horse took exception to all the people who were lined up to see the funeral procession. He said, "They acted like it was a big freak show. The Boss was our brother and his death hit all of us so hard that I could not even stay around and look at anybody too long because I would get choked up so bad."

As Ed and I looked with amazement at the crowds lining the streets, he asked me how many would line up to see us go our way. Ed glanced at a group in front of

Bikers lay leader to rest

THE MINISTER, Rev. Eugene Skipworth and his congregation watch the interment of Ronald Shelton. (Obert photo)

Coverage of Horseman funeral

us and saw his wife and mother standing, taking it all in. They were standing in front of the beauty shop down the street for their weekly appointment.

There were police cars at every intersection all the way to the cemetery. There were people standing at curbside the entire distance to the cemetery. As we entered the gates of the cemetery, we saw many police officers in plain sight with rifles and shotguns at the ready. Ed said, "Skip, this is the first committal service I have ever conducted from a crouch position."

After the casket was placed on the lowering device, everyone gathered close to hear me offer the committal prayers. After the final amen, Ed asked the cemetery workers to remove the large tent that we were under for the service because those present were going to fire a volley in tribute to The Boss. The bikers used live ammo and the tent would have been full of holes. When the tent was taken down, the bikers "showed their iron" and a tremendous volley of noise filled the air. The smoke cloud kept me from seeing all the police to catch their reaction. But, they made no gesture of retaliation. Everyone kept their cool. As they left, many waved to the police. "A lot of them waved and thanked us for being here," said Bob Steele of the Springfield Township Police. "We have an understanding between us."

When the casket was lowered, the vault was covered. Someone gave the order, probably Round, and every Horseman grabbed a shovel or used their hands to throw some dirt on the grave.

After everyone had fired up their bikes and filled up the cars, they moved away from the gravesite and out of the cemetery. Ed and I both took a big deep breath of relief. He told me, "Now, I am going to enjoy my wedding anniversary with my wife." And he did.

With some couples I was able to minister to them in pre-marital counseling. For instance, I had a specific guideline and approach for pre-marital counseling. The following is the questionnaire I used and the answers one couple gave.

PRE-MARITAL COUNSELING QUESTIONNAIRE

1. **What are the five most important factors to ensure a happy and successful marriage?**

   First...Love, Second...Children, Third...Home, Fourth...Job, Fifth...Religion

2. **Why did you name your first most important factor?**

   It is what you need to start a marriage.

3. **Have you discussed money matters after your marriage?**

   Yes, it will be handled by my wife because I spend it too fast and on nothing.

4. **Have you discussed in-laws? What did you decide?**

   Yes, and she can come over to the house any time she wants.

5. **Do you think God is necessary for your marriage and home? If so why?**

   Yes, we will have more love for our family and it will help our marriage.

6. **Why do you want to be married in a Christian Church?**

   Because I don't want to be married in a Catholic Church.

7. **Do you accept Jesus as Lord of your life? If so, why?**

   Yes, because He died for us.

8. **Has the Church been a part of your life up to now? Why or why not?**

   No, because of the friends I kept.

9. **Will the Church be a part of your married life? Why or why not?**

   Yes, because it will make it easier and God will help us with our problems.

When it came to the rare opportunity for marriage counseling, and a mama was involved, the first thing I told them was, "If you want me to help patch things up with you and your wife, you will have to forget about your mama." If the problem was drinking, I told them that had to go or they had to go to AA. In most cases, it was obvious what the problem was and I always addressed that issue first.

There were occasions when I did meet with couples who were having marital problems. It was during those opportunities that I was able to offer words of hope and guidance that a newfound relation to Christ would give. Those counseling sessions seemed to only come in moments of crisis and dire need. It was during those times that they took the initiative to call me to have such a conversation.

When those opportunities came, I tried to make them feel as welcome and comfortable as possible. I never closed the door to the office. If my kids came around, I welcomed that intrusion because it gave the couple a feel that this was a family setting, not a formal/clinical appointment. I encouraged them to bring their children. I sat in a chair facing them and did not sit behind my desk. I wanted everything to foster a relaxed conversation. I always offered them coffee or something to snack on or drink.

I always started our sessions with prayer. Then, I told them how glad I was that they came to discuss their problems. Hopefully, all this would get them both comfortable; comfortable for her because she was the one who wanted it the most and comfortable for him because it was a whole new environment for him.

I often played the role of reconciler between the bikers and the public. When they asked me to go out with them, and they suspected trouble, they would say, "Wear your collar." They didn't have to play the role of trying to get the attention of people when they had me around. When I was with them and wore my collar, we received all kinds of inquisitive looks. People would ask the bartender, "Who the hell is that preacher, and what's he doing with those guys?" One time at a bar on Columbia Parkway, some of the Cobras overheard such a comment and one of them came over to me, put his arm around me, and said, so all could hear, "Hey preacher, you had a great sermon last Sunday. I can hardly wait till next Sunday."

I was involved in a hassle with the police, which helped me become more trusted and accepted by the bikers. The hassle occurred one night when I was riding with the Cobras. Six of us pulled into the parking lot of White Castle at Harrison and Boudinot shortly after midnight. We turned off our engines and began to get off our bikes. Two off-duty police officers approached us. They began to poke some of us in the ribs with their nightsticks and told us to get off the lot. The president, Two Star, a Vietnam vet with two purple hearts, looked at me as if to say, "See, this is the crap we put up with all the time." I suggested we park in the street.

We walked up the sidewalk to go into the restaurant. The cops asked, "Where do you think you are going?" Two Star told them we were going in to eat. "Not here

Devil's Disciples provided a Chrismtas party for the Northside kids

you aren't." We went back to our bikes and the cops followed us. Someone asked "Why can't we go in and eat?" One of the cops pushed him with his night stick and made a threatening movement to another. I expected all hell to break loose. The other cop said, "Get those bikes out of here and don't come back." I was surprised when they got on their bikes and didn't make any threats, gestures, or foul language directed at the cops. We followed Two Star to a parking lot across the street.

Two Star directed his comments to me. "OK, preacher, you saw what happened. What the hell did we do wrong? What do you suggest we do now?" I told him to call the police from the phone booth on the corner and tell them to come down here and straighten out this mess. Everybody looked at each other and came to the conclusion that was a good idea.

Two Star made the phone call. We waited a long time and Two Star called a second time. Two squad cars came and they talked to the two cops at the restaurant. The police cars left and the two cops came across the street where we were. "You mother-fuckers want to complain, we'll give you something to complain about." One of them threw one of the Cobras against a wall and hit another with his stick. Still the Cobras kept their cool.

We began to get on our bikes to leave. I was the last one to roll out of the parking lot. I wanted to make sure no one did anything wrong since we were in the right and the cops had gone too far. As I slowly idled out onto the street, the cop who used his stick the most yelled in my face, "Get off that bike you mother-fucker and I'll show you what a man is really like." Then he hit me with his stick across the back of my helmet. I gassed my bike out of there.

I caught up with the rest of the Cobras and we rode to the parsonage. Everyone was outraged and wanted revenge. I suggested some of them go directly to the District Three police office to file a report. I told them I would contact Leonard Slutz, an attorney, steering committee member, and member of the Hyde Park Community United Methodist Church, to see what recourse we might have.

Mr. Slutz wrote letters to Mayor Eugene Ruehlmann, the director of safety, Colonel Henry J. Sandman, and Chief of Police Colonel Jacob Schott. He began his letter to these three gentlemen by saying, "I am much disturbed by an incident that has been brought to my attention by a young minister of my denomination. I don't know what is the best thing to do, but am convinced something should be done and am therefore seeking your opinion as to the best procedure."

About a month later, we went to court with charges against the two off-duty police officers. Mr. Slutz called me forward as a witness. I wore my collar and blue suit. The police officers did a double-take when they saw me come forward. In spite of my testimony and that of three other Cobras, the officers didn't get a slap on the wrist. Mr. Slutz wrote to Colonel Sandman on August 22, 1969 and said "I am much upset because in court the officers in question testified directly contrary to my information in at least three respects." The two police officers denied all the testimony we made against them.

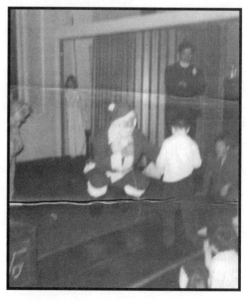

Through this experience, the word spread that I could be trusted and I became accepted by many of the outlaw motorcycle clubs.

The bikers began to "look after" the Skipworths. One time I casually mentioned to some Renegades over lunch at a White Castle in Cheviot that I needed new tires for my car. I also mentioned that my son, Yale, had seen a model airplane in a store in Northside. As the conversation continued on about kids and all that goes on in the needs of a family, I also mentioned that Nancy,

President of Devil's Disciples played Santa

my daughter, mentioned how she had seen a life-size doll at the same store and how badly she wanted one.

They never gave any indication they were paying any attention to me. The conversation went elsewhere on other subjects. The next morning I found four brand-new Shell tires on my back porch, a big model airplane, and a three-foot-tall doll. I immediately called Snake, president of the Renegades, and told him to come and get the tires off my porch and get the airplane and doll and take them back where he got them.

He said, "What you talkin' about? I ain't got time to talk to you, preacher."

"Just come and get them."

He hung up on me.

Yale had a great time with the airplane. And, Nancy loved her doll. I waited for someone to come and get the tires. One Sunday morning, during worship, someone put them on my car.

I was with the Devil's Disciples at another "social" occasion and mentioned that the church outreach committee wanted to have a Christmas party at the church for all the neighborhood kids. But, I told them we didn't have anyone to play Santa and the church had no money in the budget for gifts and candy for all the kids.

Deuce called me a few days later and told me he would play Santa and the Devil's would supply the gifts and make up stockings filled with candy for all the kids. It was one of the most successful Christmas parties our church ever provided. The old ladies and mamas came as elves and passed out stockings filled with little toy treats and candy. The Devil's passed out toys that they had not taken the time to wrap or put names on. The toys had the price tags and labels on them from one of the discount stores of that time. The women of the church provided all kinds of food and the youth fellowship of the church helped in the distribution of the treats and gifts. I have a picture in my scrapbook of Jewel Smith lining up the kids to sit on Santa's lap. The kids of Northside experienced one of their best Christmas parties ever. I know Deuce and the Devil's Disciples had a greater time and felt a great deal of pride in what they had done. The Devil's talked about the Christmas party for months afterward.

I got the expected comments from some of the people of the church the Sunday morning after the Christmas party. Joe Walton (a Korean veteran who let everyone know he was a veteran and could not stand the anti-war sentiments of so many people, and certainly could not stand the ministry to the outlaw bikers) made the first comment to me about the Christmas party. His comment was not directed to me, but loud enough for many to hear, "Well, from the looks of the carpeting and trash still lying around, it looks like Skipworth has been up to his usual stuff. We may as well turn the church building over to him and have it used for any kind of his nonsense that comes along." His wife was the one who locked her keys in her car that Grease helped unlock.

In spite of the comments from Mr. Walton and a few others, several spoke out, especially during the adult Sunday School class, with very positive comments about the Christmas party. They said, "You should have been here. I have never seen this church so alive with so many children." Jewel Smith, during the announcement time in worship, said, "I wish you all could have seen our church in action last night. There were several of us here and we have not had a finer experience. We had one of the most rewarding Christmas parties Northside has ever seen. If the Devil's Disciples ever come here for another event or worship, please let them know how much we appreciated their gift of a wonderful Christmas party."

The bikers had also built a relationship with my kids. Never once, in all the times they were in our home, did they do or say anything to hurt, embarrass, or offend us. Nancy has often marveled about the fact that having so many outlaw bikers around with their terrible reputation and frightful image, "I never saw a gun, knife, drugs, or heard them cursing when they were in our house. They always got quiet when my brother and I came around and just started talking about kid stuff, out of respect for my dad."

Nancy recalled an experience she had with some of the bikers at our house. "One night dad was at the church for a meeting. I went down in the basement where there were a bunch of bikers sitting around. They were making carvings out of soap. I watched them for a while to see what everyone was making. They told me they would let me try it but I might cut myself. I went on upstairs. Later, two of the guys came upstairs and gave me their carvings, a cross and a cat."

They would often volunteer to babysit. They learned they could come to our home anytime.

One time Weed, a member of the Midnight Drifters, came over and was eating dog biscuits and drinking Pepsi out of a 16 oz. bottle. He offered Yale a biscuit and Yale said, "That's a dog biscuit, we can't eat that."

Weed said, "Sure we can, try it."

Yale had one and told his sister how good it was. They both ate dog biscuits with Weed and they helped him finish off the Pepsi.

Yale was present in my study when Round and some other Iron Horsemen came to the house. He remembered that they seemed very upset. He heard them tell me that they had shot at a gang member of a rival club and shot a shotgun into the wrong car. The car was driven by a lady and the only thing that saved her was a part of the metal of the side window frame which stopped some of the shot.

Then, they realized they had been telling me this in front of Yale. They immediately began to apologize to me and told Yale that what they had done was really wrong, "That is why we came to tell your dad. We want to make sure the lady is OK. We want your dad to help us."

Yale said he remembers that the BIA made him a set of his own BIA colors. He said he sure wishes he still had them. What a souvenir that would be!

The bikers also became very protective of our home. Doug, an Iron Horseman, before he had his run-in with the justice system, asked, "Preacher, do you lock your doors? If you don't, you should; this is a rotten neighborhood. This place is full of thugs. You got a gun?"

"I usually lock the doors, but I don't have a gun."

"You need one. Here, take this one of mine. I got it off a Draco after I pounded him. I have another at Round's house."

"I am not going to have a gun in my house. Thanks for your concern, but I just don't want a gun."

"Don't be stupid, preacher. Take it; you got two kids to protect from the filth down here."

One of the BIA was there and told him, "We have offered him guns before. He just won't take one."

Three members of the Iron Horsemen visited us for their first time at the parsonage. As they were leaving, we told them, "We are glad to see you anytime. You are always welcome."

One of them said, "Are you telling the truth? What are your neighbors and church members going to think when we pull up on our bikes?"

Bikers began to realize that the welcome was genuine. They found they could get a meal, a cup of coffee, and conversation anytime they wanted it.

On some Sundays we would have up to four for dinner. I had a few ladies in the church ask, "Skip, do you think you will be having guests for dinner this Sunday?"

If I said yes, they always made sure we were prepared with food. Some of the bikers brought their dates, girlfriends, mamas, kids, and wives over to visit me and meet my kids.

One of the tools I had in my role as pastor and evangelist to the bikers was the picture of Jesus by J. Hook which hung on the wall of my office. I never realized it would be a good entrée to talk about Jesus; that it would get their attention. I took it for granted. I was so used to it. Whenever a biker walked into my study the picture immediately caught his eye.

"Hey, whose da bad dude?"

"That's a picture of Christ."

"What? That ain't like no pictures I seen of him. That dude is a man! He'd look good in colors. The man's righteous."

From that point we would move into a great conversation about Jesus and what kind of guy He was. I told them what He did for people, what He said. I mentioned that to most people He was a renegade and that He seemed to have trouble with the authorities. They were always interested when I told them He got thrown out of towns. They were impressed when I told them He always showed His guts and was not afraid to speak His mind. I emphasized how He came to heal people, made them whole, how He restored sight to the blind, fed the hungry, clothed the naked, and identified with the outcasts of society, how He told some "stone jags" off. But, most important, I told them that if we would allow Him to touch our lives, He could make us new persons.

My office also had a lot of posters and memorabilia of the University of Illinois, my alma mater. When they would see all my U. of I. stuff in my office, they would tease me and say, "You say you wear the colors of Jesus, that's bull. You wear the colors of the University of Illinois. Don't they call themselves the Fighting Illini? That would make a good name for a biker club. We ought to get one started, 'The Fighting Illini.' Hell, preacher, you could be the president. But, you have to get rid of the fairy colors, blue and orange."

In spite of all my efforts, I was seldom aware when and if I really got across to them. My few successes came from the most unpredictable sources.

I was visiting a biker at the hospital while he was recovering from an appendectomy. He asked me, "Did you ever get that money back from that old lady?"

"What old lady?"

"We were down in the basement of your house and a little old lady came to the window and rapped on it. She wanted to talk to you. You asked her what she wanted.

"She said she needed some money for groceries. You opened the window of the basement and gave her some money. Did you ever get it back?"

"No, I never asked anyone to give it back. They come by the house all the time wanting money for all kinds of things."

"That's what we don't understand about you, preacher. You let people take advantage of you. People use you. Sometimes we think you and your church people are not very smart."

Down deep I hoped that their trust was based on their knowledge of what mattered most to me. Crazy Horse, one of the Horsemen, told me while we were waiting in a hearse after I had conducted a funeral for the mother of one of the Horsemen, "Preacher, you must take this Jesus stuff big time. Otherwise, why would you give us the time of day? Look at us. We come to the funeral of a brother's mother dressed like cycle-trash and looking like shit. You acted like you didn't even notice. And you talked today about her 'new life' and all of us having the chance for a 'new life.' Where are you trying to go with all this?"

I told him that was not in my hands. "I don't know where God will go with this. I just know that we all have a chance to have a new and wonderful life, a life with God's hand in ours." I felt a measure of success when he remembered the phrase I used in my funeral message: "new life."

In his 1751 tract, "The Character of a Methodist," John Wesley defines Methodist character as message and mission: the blessed assurance that the Holy Spirit brings healing to the troubled soul, brings a sense of mission to the purpose-less life, and brings hope and joy irrespective of life's circumstances or the state of the world. He calls this "scriptural holiness," "the scriptural way of salvation," and the essence of "primitive Christianity."

My task was to witness to "the blessed assurance that brings healing to the troubled soul and purposeless life, and in that witness, brings hope and joy."

CHAPTER SEVEN

While I was working toward my doctoral degree at United Theological Seminary, one of my professors, Dr. Calvin Reber, suggested I invite the Iron Horsemen to the seminary. He thought it would be good to have the student body meet them and have a time for questions and answers. When I mentioned the invitation to the Iron Horsemen, some of them were skeptical. Some didn't like the idea because they thought a bunch of preachers would preach at them. Round said, "We're goin'."

We all rode up to Dayton on our motorcycles. When we drove into the seminary parking lot, many students came out to see the spectacle. They had never heard the thunder of more than twenty choppers. They never had their sanctuary invaded by such gross, disgusting, and filthy-looking persons. Aaron Sheaffer, the music director of the seminary, was one of the first to greet us. His greeting was very surprising to many of the Horsemen. They didn't expect such a smile and warm welcome.

In the assembly with the students, the Horsemen were sitting on stage in front. Most of the Horsemen were taken aback at the reception they received. Many of the students came up to them and shook their hands in a warm welcome. Many expressed their pleasure in meeting them and having them visit United. The Horsemen expected a more hostile environment with words and looks of condemnation.

Round did most of the talking after Dr. Reber welcomed them.

Round gave a presentation about motorcycle clubs and the Iron Horsemen in particular. He explained to the students what the one percenter patch on their colors meant. He said, "One percent of all bikers belong to an outlaw biker club like the Iron Horsemen. All the other 99 percent belong to the American Motorcycle Association."

Then he went on to say, "We don't hate the AMA bikers; we just don't associate with them."

The history of the Iron Horsemen was then shared. "We were established in Oxford, Ohio, in 1963. They had thirty-seven members and only two had motorcycles. Today the age limit to join is eighteen. We prefer twenty-one. You have to have a Harley Davidson motorcycle. The probation period for a prospective member is at least thirty days. We have twenty-five members today."

At this point there was a pause.

Dr. Reber asked if it would be okay for them to take questions from the students. Round said, "We really don't think that would be a good idea. Some of the answers might not be good for a bunch of preachers to hear."

Dr. Reber was insistent. He said, "We want to learn everything about you. Please feel free to say whatever you want. We need to hear it. We want to understand you."

"OK, preacher, but I warned you."

The first question was rather surprising, considering the welcome they received. It was, "Do you always try to make people afraid of you?"

Farmer John, a big intimidating figure of a man, with a beard and long hair and standing at six feet, two inches answered, "We don't. But we will never be pushed around. Especially, never push a brother. We will really fight then. No one messes with our brothers."

Another student asked, "Do you steal? We read that you break all kinds of laws, that your lifestyle is violent."

Round responded with a quick word and a bit of anger. "You have seen too many movies." After a slight pause, he seemed to settle into his usual conversation mode of being slow and deliberate. "Look, our by-laws and constitution are three and a half pages long. The constitution of the Iron Horsemen states that our objective is 'to promote motorcycling to the best interest of all its members.'"

Dr. Reber asked, "Do you have women who ride with you or can become members?"

Cutter came in with the answer which included more than what Dr. Reber asked. "Our by-laws state that 'No Afro-Americans shall be accepted as applicants.' We have women who ride with us, but they can't be members. The wives are called 'old ladies' and all the women wear a patch on their colors that state they are somebody's property. And, we have a big-time rule that no brother messes with another brother's old lady."

The next question was the one I was afraid would be asked and the one Round expected to hear. That is why he told Dr. Reber he didn't think it would be good to have a question and answer period.

A student asked, "What do all those wings mean on your colors? And the '69.'"

Crazy Horse, one of the most astute of all the Horsemen said, "You don't really want to know."

Dr. Reber came back again, "Yes, we want to know everything."

I stood up and said, "This is that line that should not be crossed. I don't think it would serve any purpose to have the question answered."

The student that asked the question, had a follow up question, "Then, what does the '13' patch mean, or is that crossing the line?"

Round said, without any hesitation, "The '13' stands for the thirteenth letter in the alphabet which is the letter 'M' which stands for marijuana. The symbols of the wings and their different colors are very personal and private to all biker groups. They have to do with oral sex, which I am sure none of you would practice. It's about stuff preachers should not hear."

A few of the students were very vocal in their feeling of disgust with the Horsemen, with the words they used, how they looked, how they acted, and what they stood for. Some of the answers were offensive to them and they said so. One student got up and walked out. None of the Horsemen said a word; it was what they expected. Later, when they talked about their experience at the seminary, in spite of the responses of some of the students, they said, "There were some righteous dudes there, especially the main man."

I could understand if some of the students were offended. But, in spite of that, in spite of the experience of meeting, seeing, and hearing the Iron Horsemen, I wondered if they saw the need to open their church doors to the outcasts of their communities. I should have asked the students to do an evaluation for me; of me, my ministry to the outlaw bikers, the Iron Horsemen, and how the church should respond. It would have been very interesting to read their responses.

Dr. Reber wanted the students to learn about the Horsemen. He was the professor of missions and recognized the need to know and understand those outside the church walls.

His grading/evaluation of my class participation in the first quarter of the 1969–1970 school year follows:

GRADUATE CLASS ON MISSIONS—DR. CALVIN REBER, PROFESSOR

I. Gene was able to open his work with the motorcycle clubs without defensiveness. His special work with the bikers requires a good and strong self-image.

II. He made the largest contribution to the class of any person through his reporting of his work with the motorcycle clubs and his asking the class for suggestions, along with his bringing the Iron Horsemen to the seminary. His own work is solidly done.

III. Gene has been able to relate well to the cycle club members-scene of his special ministry, despite the difficulty.

IV. He has developed the ability to relate well to the cycle club members and probably has more problems with some of the traditional church members. Through the denomination, he has found resources and support for this ministry.

V. This ministry requires flexibility.

VI. Gene has been seeking to maintain a clear Christian witness in his cycle ministry without needless compromises while maintaining needful contact.

VII. His membership in the class because of this work and spirit has been very stimulating to all.

Dr. Reber suggested I develop a questionnaire for the bikers to answer about their understanding of some aspects of the Christian faith. Some of their responses were:

"I believe that God is . . ."

—*A powerful, eternal, all knowing, childlike being, who can derive as much pleasure from all the complexities of a grain of sand, as he can the turmoil of sixty odd years a man spends struggling to survive.*

—*The Father of Jesus Christ. Creator of all things.*

—*Everything good and bad.*

"I believe Jesus Christ is . . ."

—Supposed to be our savior—kind of failed though!

—Intended savior of all mankind. He just needs a little more mortal help. He was God's only way to contact the people without overdoing it with sensationalism. Talking burning bushes would be hard to take blindly.

—A wonderful superhuman. He was the head instrument of a superior race. He could use a larger portion of his brain than the common man. Man can use one-tenth, Christ used nine or ten-tenths. His body had such a resistance to disease that on contact another man could be cured. He may have been able to change the molecular structure of matter by thought itself.

"I believe that creation is . . ."

—Old as time itself. The most high being in existence started the ball rolling and he has been watching ever since.

—Somebody had to make this mess. God knows it couldn't have been an accident. Man is too perfect a machine to evolve from apes.

—What's there to believe, God made it except he used Darwin's Theory.

"I believe the church is . . ."

—A bunch of pious clowns hung up on a shot theory.

—One of the most hypocritical organizations around today. Granted there are some good Christians, but there are a hell of a lot more who are as two-faced as Judas. In fact, that is a good name for them, "a twentieth century Judas."

—A faulty instrument of man used to better his kind. Churches have caused as many senseless deaths as disease. There have always been too many ignorant, hypocritical, polar thinkers as heads of churches.

—Hell is composed of fire and brimstone. (Ask any Baptist.)

"I believe the purpose of life is . . ."

—To survive for yourself first, your loved ones second.

—Life is man's chance to make up his mind between heaven and hell. He does it all himself. Therefore, there should be no reason for deathbed repentance.

—No free will! God knows everything. Even though you have a choice he knows which you'll choose. No free will!

"I believe the resurrection is . . ."

—Wow! Really great if you can pull it off.

—The only way Christianity could have survived. If there hadn't been a resurrection, God would have truly been dead.

—Christ had a look-a-like. His human body healed itself after the heart stopped. Or, the resurrection was just so much shit handed down mouth to mouth.

"I believe sin is . . ."

—The ten commandments sum that up perfectly. No ninety I. Q. wrote those.

—The choices between heaven or hell.

—What other people think is wrong.

"I believe forgiveness is . . ."

—When you say to yourself, its o.k.

—A basic essential for Christianity. Man has a choice. If he makes the wrong one,

but realizes it in time, he deserves the right to prove his loyalty to God. These people are truly the best Christians.

—Time and the ability to forget.

"I believe the death of Christ is . . ."

—He accomplished his goal and died in doing so.

—God's way to prove to the people his loyalty and love toward them. After all, even if you do know he's coming back to life, it's still hard to watch your son suffer. Besides, his suffering gave the poor something to identify with.

—A sad story about a perfect guy.

I learned a great deal about the religious beliefs and non-beliefs of the bikers from the many hours of conversation and questions they raised about the Bible, the church, and religion. I found that their backgrounds and experiences of growing up in some churches determined their attitude about religion. To better understand and show compassion, I needed to listen to their heartache and longing. I needed to try to look into their eyes and spirits and see the depth of their need. I needed to really hear what they had to say about their own prospects for hope.

Fats was about twenty years old and a member of the Fugueros. It was easy to see how he got his name; he was short, chubby, and had a baby's complexion. He hardly ever spoke to me. He always had a surly look on his face when he looked at me. He always seemed defensive with me with a chip on his shoulder. His sister, Wanda, (who wore the patch "Property of Tonto") told me why Fats was so mean and against religion. She said that when he was growing up and did something wrong, their mother would make him stand and read the Ten Commandments off a plaque on the living room wall while she spanked him with a short broom handle. One time, when he was about eight years old and during one of the "righteous" beatings, Fats placed his hands over his backside to protect himself from his mother's blows and she broke his little finger. Fats never wanted me to ride with the Fugueros and always showed a belligerent attitude toward me when I came around.

When I first got acquainted with the Brothers In Arms, Blackie always kept his distance from me. He was about six feet, three inches and had a slim build. When the BIA came to the house for their meetings in the basement, he never came upstairs after the meetings to visit with the rest of the guys. After the meetings, he left right away. He never set foot in the church except on the last night of the Lenten studies. He never had anything good to say about religion and the church.

One day, Sarge brought him to the house with the assurance that it was okay to talk to me. "He won't say anything to anybody." Sarge was one of the first outlaw bikers to attend worship. Sarge joined the Marines and wrote to me often. (I've included two of his letters.) When he came to visit while on leave, he looked great in his uniform, short hair, and cleanly shaven face. On one leave, he brought his wife to meet me. They were married in her church. Sarge, in our many conversations, never expressed any animosity toward the church as most bikers did.

After some awkward silence, Sarge said, tell Skip what you told me. Blackie said, "My mom made me go to a Sunday school at a church down the street when I was a kid. During Sunday school, I had to go to the bathroom and the teacher wouldn't let me go. She said I just wanted to cause trouble. I pissed my pants and she made me sit there the whole time. She even laughed at me. I don't hate you, Skip, I just don't like the church and the people in the church."

I was not surprised about the views some of the bikers like Fats and Blackie had toward Christ and the church. While there were a few who would not trust me or want to be around me, many of the bikers were very willing to talk and listen when religion was brought up. Farmer John expressed their interest one night when I was getting ready to go home after a lengthy discussion at Cutter's apartment. "Hey, preacher, don't leave now, we are just getting into this thing. You may get some converts out of us yet. I doubt it, but you might."

It was very refreshing to have discussions with bikers who were genuinely searching for some affirmation about life. One such biker was Deuce of the Devil's Disciples. Deuce was the only outlaw biker I met that most closely fit the image of the American Motorcycle Association biker. He looked like a professional of some sort. He wore short hair and a well-trimmed beard. He had a positive outlook on life, was not defensive, did not have a chip on his shoulder, and never used profane or vulgar language. He had a steady job for over five years. He had a lovely wife and two children. He was devoted to his family. I never got the idea that the Devil's Disciples came before his family.

Each time I was with the Devil's, he would get me off to the side where we could really get into a deep conversation about religion. I learned that he had read some theology, and had an understanding of world religions and philosophy.

Once I visited him in the hospital when he was recovering from a broken leg from a bike accident. In our conversation, I was surprised to learn he was reading *Chariots of the Gods?* by Erich von Däniken. Several million copies had been sold. The book suggests that Earth may have been visited repeatedly by aliens from other worlds. Deuce said, "I can't conceive of such ideas. I compare it to some of the other readings from theologians like Leslie Weatherhead and his book, *The Christian Agnostic*, where he talks about predestination, providence and care, and authority." He recommended I get the book *Chariots of the Gods?* so that we might discuss it. I gladly did so. I never before had a biker recommend a book for me to read.

While Deuce was home recovering, I brought him a Bible and I shared with him some of the gems of what Jesus said. Deuce became acquainted with the Beatitudes and especially the words of Jesus about having a life in all its abundance. I shared the five texts where Jesus mentioned why he came. Deuce was one of the few who made it easy to plant the seed of Christ's love.

Deuce, Filthy Phil, Sarge, and most of the bikers would be cordial and courteous when a church member would drop by the parsonage. Some of the more active lay people were very popular with some of the bikers. Jewel Smith always got hugs from those grubby "teddy bears," as she called them. Mr. Whitekamp, a long-time church member, trustee, and resident of Northside, all five-feet-one-inch of him, often got engulfed by huge hugs. Mr. Whitekamp had three daughters and the bikers always teased him about taking them out for rides on their bikes. Each of his daughters was old enough to be their mothers.

The bikers seemed to know who their friends were from the NUMC and those who didn't want them around. They came to know that not everyone in the church supported me and that some wanted me to leave. But, they would do anything for a member of the NUMC because they felt accepted by so many of the members.

One day a few Horsemen were visiting me at the parsonage and I received a phone call from one of the parishioners who had not been in favor of my ministry to the bikers. He had just received a phone call from someone who lived near the church who told him there were several motorcycles parked in front of the church. The caller told me to tell them to leave. I didn't.

After I hung up the phone, I told the Horsemen about the call. I told them that some of the church members still did not want me to associate with them and wanted the district superintendent to move me.

Telling those few Horsemen I was having trouble with some members of the church turned out to be a mistake. They told Round and he called a mandatory to go to the district superintendent's office in downtown Cincinnati. They took great pride as they recounted the dialogue which took place in the office. More than twenty of them walked in the office and faced Edith, the secretary.

Edith had served as the secretary for the district for several years. If there was any question regarding any church or clergy person, Edith had the answer. At district meetings, Edith sat quietly out of the limelight taking the minutes and answering any question that called for clarity. She was a very quiet lady, about five feet tall, middle-aged, slender in build, and wore her hair in a bun. She looked like the typical librarian. Every time I was at the district office for business, she seemed very reserved and all business. I never heard her speak about a husband or family. It was as if her whole life centered on her work. She was an important and dedicated employee of the church. I am sure she was never late for work and the last one to leave.

She was busy at her desk and did not immediately see the build-up of such a hulking, intimidating, and overpowering presence of intruders. Round said that when she looked up and saw everyone, she looked as if she were in shock.

He said, "Is this the place of the guy in charge of Methodist preachers?"

"Yes."

"Does he know a preacher named Skip?"

"Yes."

"Does he know some of those people in the preacher's church want him moved?"

"Yes."

"We want to talk to the man."

"He is not here right now. Would you like to leave a message?"

"Yeah."

Edith got out her note pad to take the message.

Round said, "Tell the man that if he moves the preacher, we will burn the church down."

Big Mike, one of the Horsemen who recounted the dialogue, said the secretary stopped writing and looked up from her note pad with her eyes wide open. She looked scared and asked in a nervous voice, "Anything else?"

Nothing else was said. The Horsemen just slowly walked out the door.

About two hours later, I received a phone call from the district superintendent, Dr. Brown. He told me Edith told him about the visit with the Horsemen. He asked, "They don't mean to do any harm do they?" I told him they just dropped off four three-gallon cans of gasoline in my garage that afternoon. He said, "Skip, you know we are not going to move you. Your ministry is very important to the district and conference. Tell them to call me so I can assure them that you will not be moved. I also want to tell them that threatening to burn down a church is not the way to get their point across. I may make them angry when I talk to them, but I want to tell them that I did not appreciate the way they came in the office."

I told him that whatever he wanted to say to them would be welcomed by me. I also told him I would have Round apologize to Edith for their abruptness.

Round called Dr. Brown and told him there would be no church burning. Round asked him, "Do you want us to come to any meeting at the church to set anybody straight?"

Dr. Brown told him that everything was taken care of. But, he added, he wanted Round to talk to Edith and apologize for the abrupt way the Horsemen came into the office.

Round told me he asked Dr. Brown to give the phone to Edith and Round said he apologized to her. Round said, "I told her we were sorry and if she ever needed anything, all she had to do was call me." He gave Edith his number.

Soon after this incident, Big Mike showed up at worship by himself. I was very surprised to see him. He wore his colors, but was seated in the back where no one would notice him. He was always quiet, always a follower, and never seemed to take the initiative to do anything on his own. In spite of being called "Big Mike," he was not big at all. When I saw him in worship, I wondered, *Oh no, now what?*

Most churches have welcome cards for visitors to fill out which are located in a small slot next to the hymnal racks. In addition to the welcome cards, there are offering envelopes. Big Mike participated in worship and spoke to some of the members on his way out.

After worship, one of the ushers handed me a welcome card filled out by Big Mike. The card's message was typical of all the welcome cards churches use. "WELCOME . . . To the Worship and Fellowship of Northside United Methodist Church. If we can be of service to you, please check in the space below and deposit this card with your offering, or hand it to an usher. Requests for prayers or other messages may be written on the other side." There were spaces for the name, address, phone number, and date at the top of the card. Underneath were eight small boxes for a person to check which included "I am a newcomer to this community," "I would appreciate a call from the minister," "I have moved to the new address noted above." There were five other boxes to check. Big Mike added another box, checked it, and wrote, "See back."

On the back he had written;

I think by sending Gene Skipworth out of this church to find another you is making the biggest mistake of your lives. Gene has young ideas. He can make this parish the young people center of Cincinnati. He is young. He acts young. He lets others see fun and Christ can walk hand in hand. Skip is open to criticism but please criticize him openly. Don't condemn a man with as much potential for the young as Billy Graham has for the multitude he reaches. God please forgive those who blindly judge a Christian by his dress or hobbies. Thank you. Amen.

There were some experiences with other bikers that gave me the feeling that my prayers were being answered, that Christ was making some headway in some of their lives, and that my ministry was making some impact.

J. D., a Renegade, wanted to go with me to make some house calls on some of my shut-ins.

"J. D., if you walk into a room of one of those ladies wearing your colors, she will be shocked. She would tell us both to get out."

"I won't wear my colors. I just want to go and see what you do."

We went. He didn't wear his colors, he combed his hair, and wore regular street clothes rather than jeans and boots. He couldn't get over the first visitor's question, "Are you Reverend Skipworth's assistant?"

"Yes, madam, I'm helping him make some of his calls. He is very busy and he asks me to help him out sometimes."

We visited for a while and as we were getting ready to leave, I asked, "J. D., would you like to offer a prayer before we leave?"

Without missing a beat, he said, "Yes. Peace and love to you, ma'am. Amen."

He said he could hardly wait to go back to the church and tell some of the people of the church what he had done. He wouldn't dare tell his brothers of the Renegades what he had done!

I seemed to have more success with the BIA. Maybe it was because they were a Northside biker club and many of them lived near the parsonage. Buzz was one of those BIA who lived down the street from the church. I saw him change gradually while a member of the BIA. He spent a lot of time at our house. On many Sundays after church, he would join us for dinner and talk about the sermon. He became one of the more regular attendees at worship. He arrived early and became acquainted with many of the church members. He helped with the breakfast program and the after-school tutoring program.

Eventually, at one of their meetings, he took off his colors and threw them on the floor and told the rest of the club to shove them. He went upstairs to the living room and watched television with the kids. That was his "coming out."

He became a member of the BIA on the merits of his fighting ability. He was strong and unafraid of anything or anyone. When he was voted into the BIA, no one voted against him. He usually had little or nothing to say at the meetings. When he did talk, everyone listened. After he dropped out of the BIA, no one gave him any hassle.

Buzz wanted to be baptized and join the church. After he did, he held an office in the church and became one of my closest friends and supporters in the church.

Another one of those persons was Sarge. He was called Sarge because he always told everybody what to do and he was big enough to get by with it. He was six feet, four inches tall, muscular, handsome, had long blond hair, but very wild. Crazy might be a better word. He jumped off a bridge into the Ohio River on a dare of a fellow BIA. He challenged four Outcasts, armed only with a knife, to a fight. He cut one and the others took off. He often rode his motorcycle with no brakes and would take any kind of pill that anybody had as his stupid way to show he had guts.

When I first met Sarge, he had just joined the BIA. Two older members of the club brought him by the house to meet me. They introduced us and before I could say, "Hello, glad to meet you," he said, "Preacher, don't give me no shit about God and church. Save it for all those jags that you see on Sunday mornings. Don't ever lay that shit on me, ever. You hear me, man?"

I said, "Yes," hoping he would not stop in too often.

One night a few of the BIA came over to lift weights with me. After I finished my workout, they stayed on to talk, lift, watch TV, and just carry on. Sarge was with them.

They kept me up most of the night with their noise. I was kind of angry when I came downstairs the next morning. I was putting on my shoes in the living room while

123

they were watching cartoons with my kids. I told the kids to go upstairs and get dressed and get ready for school. I said to Sarge, "Sarge, you say there is no God, right?"

"Yeah, you got it right, preacher."

"You said for me to never talk to you about God, right?"

"Right again, preacher."

"Well, let me tell you something. There is a God and that God is a God of love and if it wasn't for that God of love in my life I would have come downstairs last night and beat the crap out of you. Do you hear me, man?" I had no idea what response I would get from him or the others; I was too angry to care. Sarge looked at me like I was crazy and the others quickly turned back to the television as if they were trying to tune out what they just heard.

I invited them to join the kids and me for coffee and breakfast. They all joined us, even Sarge. They started buttering their toast and I said, "We are going to have prayer first and if you don't like it you can leave."

They all looked at Sarge and when he bowed his head, they did, too. It was one of the most rewarding moments in my whole ministry to the bikers.

As weeks went on, Sarge spent more and more time at the house. He babysat for me when I had meetings at the church or when I had hospital calls to make. He started coming to church. He was one of the first BIA to attend regularly. Most often he came in late and sometimes he staggered in. But he never wore his colors to church. He eventually saw that belonging to an outlaw biker club was not for him. He left the BIA and joined the Marines.

Following are two letters from Sarge while he was serving in the Marine Corps. In his first letter, dated September 1969, he wrote:

Hi Skip,

How are ya's? Say, Skip, you know I couldn't forget to write one of my few true friends. I have a little time so I thought I'd drop a couple of lines. How's your bike looking?

Guess what man? Me and Janet are getting engaged probably in Dec. and hitched when I get back from Vietnam (13 months).

In the meantime we can pack the money away (What money?).

Tell me what you think. I'd like to have you marry us but I think she's hung up on a Catholic wedding. Give me a little married facts and advice. Okay?

124

Man this place is rougher than holy hell (sorry man). Always on the move. Hey I got to go now. Give me a couple lines if you have time.

Ex-cycle-trash, Sarge

P.S. Hey Skip! You'll never guess in a million years who's in my platoon. James Miller (ex Brother In Arms) Small world.

P.S. Please give Janet a ring on the phone and tell her to go to your church or just talk to her because she thinks a lot of you. (Well maybe a little?)

P.S. If you see that Carol ("Chopper girl") don't give her my address. OK?

The second letter was dated February 15, 1970.

Hi Skip,

How's you man and the kids doing? Man I'm real sorry I never been keeping in touch with you. I hope you understand how it is in this fucked up Marine Corps. They keep me real busy. I was home on a 20 day leave over Christmas. I never had any wheels to stop down and my buddies didn't want to. I don't want you to think I'm a prick—well, maybe I am. Ha!

How's your bike looking? Are you riding with the Cobras? Tell them hi. OK?

I've been in training and school for 5 months. I'm finally permanent personnel at "29 Palms Calif." in the middle of the "Mahavi Desert." When I finished communications school I had orders for Nam but they were changed to here. It didn't break my heart because I've seen too many marines that have been to Nam and they came back butchered up.

Guess what man? I put the old engagement ring on Janet. I'm going to try to marry her in a year or less, if I can swing it financially. I's appreciate it if you'd give me some of your professional advice—like how much to start with (money). I make $127.80 a month and would get an extra $100 a month for a wife. Let me know if you think I can make it. I respect your advice whether it makes me feel good or bad.

My hair is a whole 2" now. Ha! I'm finally allowed to grow a mustache. I can start looking like my old grotesque self again. Ha!

Is Filthy Phil still hanging around Northside? Remember "Goofy" the ex Brother In Arms? Well, he got married to some chick that was already knocked up. Not by him either. I hope he knows what he is doing.

My brother's wife Nancy and the kids are doing fine. She bought an expensive home. I don't know how the hell she does it. Look Skip I think I'll hit the rack now. It's pretty late. Take care and write back if you have time.

P.S. I would really dig it if you would marry me and Janet. She's digging on a fancy Catholic wedding though. Maybe if I knock her around a little she would see things my way. Ha! Just kidding!

P.S.S. I beat the piss out of my buddy, Cong Killer. He was dancing with Janet at a party at my brothers when I was on leave. He had the balls to pull up her dress. Man, I tore his ass 10 different ways.

P.S.S.S. Sorry about the long p.s.'s Ha!

On one of his leaves he and Janet were married. The kids and I took them out for dinner and this big marine dressed up in his uniform, said, with tears in his eyes, "Skip, thanks for getting involved in my life." My son, Yale, who later joined the army and became a paratrooper with the 82nd airborne, said, at the time, what a difference he saw in Sarge and how great he looked in his uniform.

My daughter mentioned that more than twenty years after my ministry to the bikers, she would see some of them, and when they recognized who she was, they would tell her "It was your daddy's influence that helped turn my life around."

Nancy said she had met so many who told her that her daddy had helped them become sober and clean and she mentioned that a couple of the former bikers had even started their own businesses.

Nancy told me about her contact with one of the bikers while she was in the Air Force. "One very special biker to me was Squirrel who has long since been dead. When I was in the Air Force and stationed in San Antonio, Texas, he had moved from Cincinnati to Dallas/Ft. Worth and opened his own custom Harley-Davidson shop. He would drive down to San Antonio on some weekends and take my daughter and me to the zoo or the park or out to eat. He was always looking out for 'Preacher Skip's baby girl.'"

Filthy Phil was one of the most engaging, interesting, and captivating personalities that I encountered in my ministry to the outlaw bikers. To this day, he and I treasure our experiences and mutual love for each other. He has always been so very close to my heart. He truly became a child of God. I do not know why he was called Filthy Phil. He was not a filthy person. He did not speak with a filthy mouth. His name was not Phil.

I first met him in the encounter with the Brothers In Arms. He was only about five feet, nine inches and weighed about one hundred fifty. He was fearless. In his few years as a biker, he had his jaw and some other bones broken. He had a bullet lodged in his right thigh for over a year and another one in his left shoulder blade. He had been in more fist fights, knife fights, and gun battles than any biker I had met. Underneath that rough, unpredictable, hyperactive, and often weird behavior was a young man with talent and the capacity to be sensitive and understanding.

The BIA was the first biker club with which I became involved and Filthy Phil was one of the first bikers that I got close to. He spent a lot of time in our home and became close to my kids. He was the favorite babysitter of my kids.

He told me, in one of our many conversations, that he would like to live with us. I told him, "If you change, get a part-time job, go back and finish school, stay away from some of your friends and the BIA, stay away from those girls you hang around with, get a nice girlfriend, don't mess with all the drugs and booze, stop smoking, wear clean neat clothes, keep your room neat, and your body clean, you can live here."

He looked hurt and said, "I would really like to live here with you and Yale and Nancy, but I just couldn't do all that stuff."

I am sure he felt hurt from what I said. He saw the way I looked on him as a person. He didn't say it but I could imagine him saying, "You only care for me, if . . ." He was beginning to trust me and I ruined that by looking at him like everyone else looked at him.

It was from that experience with Phil that I began to look more closely at the bikers from the inside and not the outward appearance. The very thing I preached against, I was becoming guilty of doing myself. I was now wanting to change the bikers into a neat-looking, middle-class image of myself. I was slipping into the redneck cliché of "Get them a bar of soap and cut their hair." I was not accepting them and loving them as Jesus did the outcasts of society. The imagined response I thought Filthy was giving me, "You only care for me if I do certain things and look different," was a needed readjustment of the way I was looking at bikers. I had hurt Filthy and it taught me a great deal about looking at the "inside of the cup" and not the "outside."

I confessed to him that I blew it. I told him that I hoped he would give me another chance. He continued to come around and continued to become a part of the life of the Skipworth family. But, he never talked about living with us again.

As time went on, Filthy became more and more in tune with a new role for his life. He saw and heard people in the NUMC; how they treated each other, how they embraced him and the other bikers, how they showed, through the ministries of the church, that love and compassion to others were more important than anything else the church should do. He also experienced the realization, that in so many ways, he was becoming different from his brothers of the BIA and bikers from other clubs.

He learned to curb his anger, he stopped getting into fights, he began to think before he acted, and showed that he really considered the interests of others. He

became close to members of the church and often asked them if he could be of help to them. He always wanted to help me with the kids. If one would ask my kids who babysat the most and who they preferred, they would say Filthy Phil.

I read a book on the pony express, *The Saga of the Pony Express*, by Joseph J. De Certo. As De Certo described the young men who were recruited for riders, I immediately thought of Filthy Phil. He would have made an excellent rider for the pony express. The ad for the riders said, "Wanted, young, skinny, wiry fellows. Must be expert riders, willing to risk death daily. Orphans preferred." The author described one rider, Jack Keetly, as a sturdy young man who routinely performed extraor-

Filthy Phil mows the parsonage lawn

dinary tasks. De Certo wrote:

He had incredible stamina, as he illustrated with one mail run that few other riders could match. After completing his normal eastbound run, due to some unknown circumstances, presumably a missing or indisposed relief rider, he agreed to make the next run, nearly a two hundred mile ride.

The pony express riders had to outrun bandits and Indians, ride through extreme weather conditions including scorching heat and snow storms. De Certo wrote that the young, fearless riders signed up enthusiastically for this challenge of being a pony express rider. I could see Filthy Phil eagerly accepting such a challenge.

Filthy Phil (Gary Boyd) after conversion at Cincinnati Bible College

When we were alone, he would talk to me about his family. He had a father, and although his father lived in Northside, he only saw him about twice a year. He was hungry for the acceptance, love, and guidance that only a father could give. He brought up all the trouble he had been in, the kind of friends he had, and the lack of direction he had for his life. He mentioned that the one thing he wanted to do more than anything else was be a big brother to a young boy; to prevent him from turning out to be another Filthy Phil.

The BIA had their meetings in the parsonage basement. After the meetings, we would lift weights and they would stay and we would talk until late in the night. During one of the Tuesday night meetings, I invited them to the weekly Lenten Bible study at the church. The first night of the study, Filthy was the only one to attend. At the next meeting of the BIA, he told them that he was not going to be the only one to attend the study sessions; they better be at the next one. For the next study, about a dozen showed up for the potluck. After the potluck, we heard a lot of Harley Davidsons take off from Delaney Street next to the church. Filthy was the only one who stayed for the study.

At the next BIA meeting, Filthy gave them an ultimatum, "If you come to the potluck, you stay for the Bible study." The next time they all stayed.

When I asked if anyone wanted to offer the prayer of blessing before our dinner, one of the lay persons would volunteer or I would. One evening I asked if anyone would like to offer our grace and Filthy, out of the clear blue sky said, "I'm going to pray, man." Before I could say "OK," he started. "God, thanks for the food and these people. Amen." His Brothers seemed more surprised than anyone.

"What the hell. Hey, man, you gonna be a preacher?"

"The dude's got religion."

"Take an offering, Phil." Everybody was laughing, but Filthy.

He said, "Knock off the crap, I wanted to pray. You ought to try it sometime."

Filthy's daughter, Tracie, while attending the University of Cincinnati, wrote the following paper for one of her English classes.

A Day in the Life of a Biker Child

It wasn't until I was older when I discovered that not all daddys in the world rode Harley Davidsons. Still to this day, a group of bikers my daddy used to belong to, refer to me as a "biker child." Along with all the other children, you could say I was spoiled rotten when it came to love and attention.

All decked out in leather and tattoos, my daddy was my hero. Although my parents had divorced when I was young and my mother received custody, I still spent a lot of time with my daddy.

There had been countless times when I would receive a telephone call saying that he was on his way, to be ready to hit the open road. I remember running around in excitement, trying to find the perfect riding pants. Sitting on our second story porch in my pea-green polyester high-water pants, I could hear the rumble and feel the thunder beneath my feet, even though he was blocks away. He was coming to get me.

As the rumble came closer and closer, I would stand up on the chair so I could see the top of the street. Holding my hands over my eyes to block the sun, there it was, glistening in the sunlight as lightning would in the night, 25 to 30 iron horses with my daddy leading the pack. You could look around and see all the neighbors standing on their porches, calling their children inside, watching with fearful eyes, and some even holding their ears. Then they would look over and see me, this little

girl, come running out of the house and hop on the back of this Harley Davidson and race off like a bolt of lightning through the sky.

With all the different places we would ride to and all the sights my little eyes could see, I experienced the beauty of the open road. Feeling as if I were a little princess who was protected by all her knights on their shiny horses, this was the community I was brought up in, a community made up of motorcycles, love and leather.

The older I got the more I realized that the biker lifestyle was one big party, the kind of party that is full of fun and free spirits. Bikers are known by onlookers to be mean, rude, and violent seeking people. I am not saying that this observation is not true, but the community of which I was a part was not in that particular category.

Being such a young girl at this time in my life, I can say that there was not a safer place to be than with my daddy and his friends. They treated all of us children as if we were the most important people on this earth. Now that I am an adult, I realize that we were. These men and women, whom all of us children called aunts and uncles, were very caring and loving toward us. From piggy back rides to wiping away tears, what more could a kid ask for? I guess you could say that I had two families, one who dressed in all leather and one who dressed in cotton. I had a taste of both worlds and loved every minute of it.

It upsets me that onlookers for years now have stereotyped bikers just because they are different from them. Being on the outside of this certain community, I can, however understand their fears. But I'm from the inside and know first hand that these big, hairy, tattooed brutes are as soft as teddy bears. Yes, it is true when it is said that these bikers can be mean, but only when it comes to defending their family. All in all, bikers are a group of big-hearted men and women.

After so many years, today I occasionally bump into some of the older bikers that I knew as a little girl, and sure enough they remember me. Like all the other children, we were given nicknames. Mine, "Button," was given to me by my uncle Red when I was five years old.

Although my daddy is no longer riding with his friends, they will always be a family to him and myself. I carry "biker blood" in my veins and always in my heart. I believe it is true when it's said that your childhood memories and experiences are with you forever. Being a biker child in today's society has actually helped me to learn how to have an open mind about things and the people around me. I am able

to see the good in all and the beauty in everything. And one thing is for sure, I do
know how to party!

The summer of 1969, I was dean at Camp Sabina, a junior high church camp of the West Ohio Conference of the United Methodist Church. A few weeks before the camp began, I talked to Filthy about coming to the camp to tell his story. He was hesitant and said he wouldn't know what to say. I told him just to be himself and tell the kids not to make the same mistakes he made.

When he made his loud grand entrance on his chopper onto the camp grounds, everything stopped and all the kids went straight to him. Kids and counselors gathered around him and his bike. Most of them had never seen a motorcycle club member and his bike. It was like a celebrity had just arrived. He had not cleaned up for the occasion. He had not shaved, combed his long hair, changed clothes, put on deodorant, or looked like he was going to speak to the youth of a church camp. He had ridden over one hundred miles to be there and he looked it.

I only promised him dinner, breakfast, and a bunk bed in the dorm where all the boys slept if he came to visit. He was only going to be there one day and one night. He enjoyed the experience so much; he ended up spending the rest of the week. The kids loved him. He enjoyed the worship services, the music, the camp grounds, and the whole new experience of a church camp. It was all new to him. He said when we sang "Amazing Grace" around the campfire, he really thought he ought to stay longer than the one day and night.

During dinner, all the kids wanted to sit at his table and talk to him. They wanted to hold his helmet. They wanted to hear everything he said. They wanted him to show them his bike. They wanted him to start his bike so they could hear the power and loudness. Filthy Phil loved every minute of it. He also knew why he was there and he assured me and some of the other counselors that he knew his responsibility.

We sat around a campfire. About ninety junior high youth were there and about ten counselors. I introduced him as a member of the Brothers In Arms motorcycle club. I told them that he had begun to learn about Christ and had joined the Northside United Methodist Church. I told them he was responsible for getting the Brothers In Arms to come to the church and attend the Lenten Bible study.

Filthy told the kids, "I hope you don't judge me by the way I look. I know I don't look as good as you. But I ain't a bad person. Oh, I done some bad things. But I don't anymore. You don't know how lucky you are to have a good home, go to school, and get to come to a place like this and learn about Jesus. Don't be stupid like me and the other Brothers."

He told them he wished he had learned sooner about Jesus. He said he found a lot of people at the church who really liked him. The kids were quiet and paid close attention to everything he said. Filthy's confidence began to rise.

When the opportunity came for the kids to ask questions, most of them were about the Brothers In Arms, his colors, his bike, how many times he had been shot, how many times he had been in jail, how many fights he had been in, and what the Brothers In Arms did when they went on a "run." He maneuvered his way through the questions in such a way that the kids saw the new and true Filthy Phil. I served as dean of church camps sixteen times in my thirty five years in the ministry. The experience at Camp Sabina was the best of them all because of Filthy Phil's presence.

When I served as pastor of Church of the Savior in Montgomery, Ohio, a suburb of Cincinnati, Filthy spoke to our congregation on a Stewardship Sunday. It was thirty years after his presentation at the church camp at Camp Sabina. He spoke about his life as a biker and his values then. He was very honest and straightforward about his mistakes and the lack of direction for his life.

His message was one of second chances. He emphasized giving to God in return for all he has given to us as a symbol of having a second chance. He spoke about the need to give to the church so that Christ could get things done here and now. When Filthy Phil was awarded ten thousand dollars in a social security settlement, he tithed ten percent to his church. Filthy is a devout member of a Nazarene Church on the west side of Cincinnati.

Filthy Phil, Sarge, Buzz, Deuce, Pud, Flake, Cisco, and others made me feel everything was worthwhile; the threats, the fear I felt, the yellow streak down my back that seemed to grow more and more, the tough questions, the lack of significant answers, the late hours, being away from my kids, hassles with cops and outlaw bikers, the failures, frustrations, the lack of a positive response from guys I thought were really coming along, having Walt tell me that he used to think that the gang was where it was at but finding out later it wasn't, having Cutter spend some evenings with me at church meetings and tell me how hanging around me and some of the church people really changed him, and having Steve spill his guts to me one night about what a fool he had made of himself and a mess of his family and how he made me feel when he said, "You are the only one who can help me put it all back together again."

133

I felt I had some measure of success when bikers would call me at all hours of the day and night wanting me to come and see them and help them in a time of crisis. I felt the message was getting across when they began to put their trust in me, confided in me, and wanted me to be there when their families faced serious issues. When those experiences took place during those three years, it made me feel they were responding to Christ's love.

I remember the date very well when Farmer John called and told me, after six years in the Iron Horsemen, he had dropped out. It was April 18, 1975. He said, "I know how much you cared and that's why I wanted you to be the first to know that I've dropped out of the Iron Horsemen."

When I had former outlaw biker club members call me, come and visit, and unexpectedly drop in for worship, it was always a special thrill. When they called and wanted me to visit a sick friend or relative of theirs, it meant that they must have received some help from me at one time and appreciated what I was trying to do. When they would call and want me to perform a wedding for them, that was very meaningful to me, especially when it was a former biker and his mama.

CHAPTER EIGHT

The steering committee was a great help in the ministry to the many motorcycle clubs. Leonard Slutz, one of the attorneys on the committee, provided advice, counsel, and represented some of the club members when they needed an attorney. There were many situations that could have had serious repercussions for me personally. I was glad I had the help and advice of the steering committee when I was confronted with difficult problems.

A common problem I had was being suspected by a club when one of their members encountered problems with the law. While one of the Gladiators, Ice, was on probation, he was locked up for causing a fight and disturbing the peace. I happened to be at the bar with two other Gladiators when he got in the fight. After the fight, they all left. The bar owner and the two men the Gladiator got in a fight with, called the police. Soon afterward, the police found him at his house and arrested him for violation of his probation.

The Gladiators sent a "rustler" to visit me. The intent of a rustler is to get a feel or check out a suspicion the club might have of someone. Some of the Gladiators thought I had called the police and told them where Ice lived. The rustler probed me with all kinds of questions: did I know that Ice had been arrested for violation of his probation? Had I been at the bar when the police arrived? Did I know where Ice lived? Where had I gone after the fight? Whom had I talked to after I left the bar?

I had the pressure taken off me when his mother told them she was the one who called the police. I thought I had the trust and confidence of the Gladiators, but experiences like that always made me feel uneasy and vulnerable.

I encountered another problem which could have had serious repercussions for me. It was when the FBI raided the homes of some of the Iron Horsemen and found several weapons, including a machine gun. An Iron Horseman told me about it the day after it happened. I worried what would happen to me if Round or some of the other Horsemen thought I notified the FBI. I went over to his house immediately after I found out. Round wasn't home, but I asked his wife what the result of the raid was. She told me that a rival club member squealed on a couple of the Horsemen.

I came out okay from that situation, which could have put me in real danger. As I began to be more trusted by the different clubs, those issues became less of a problem for me. I was convinced of that trust when they began to give me all kinds of confidential information. It was as if I was their Father Confessor. Having the steering committee available to listen to and give counsel to me when I had such "off the record" information gave me a great deal of assurance.

I wasn't ready for the different tests they put me through. One test they took a great delight in was having one of their mamas test me to see if I would forget what I preached to them about their undisciplined sex life. A mama would turn on her "I never made it with a preacher before" routine.

Their mamas, old ladies, and girlfriends (groupies) fit the stereotype of a biker mama very well. A colleague friend of mine, who attended a biker wedding I had, described them as having "been around the block a few times." Many of them liked their booze, drugs, and kinky, lewd, wild sex. Most of them had great bodies, were sexy looking and liked to show it. A biker would not be caught dead with a woman who was not attractive to all the other bikers.

The mamas and ladies who rode and hung out with the bikers had long, stringy hair that was colored black, red, or blond. They often would wear a leather, belt-like strap around their foreheads that was used as a bandana and it had leather braids or straps that hung down along their backs. They never wore make-up. They did not mind being passed around the barroom if that was what it took to get into the action and booze and drugs. They always wore boots, but seldom underwear. They wore sunglasses. They wore the colors of the club they rode with and their colors would say, "Property of . . ." They didn't wear bras and their tops under their colors were sleeveless with a lot of cleavage showing. Most wore tight tee shirts. When they wore blue denim sleeveless tops with a collar, they buttoned one button and tied a knot with the two corners of the bottom of the blouse. In the fifties we called it a "Daisy Mae," but in those days there wasn't as much revealed. They wore jeans with bell bottoms that were so tight they looked like they grew into them. Their jeans revealed their navels long before it became popular in the late 90s. They tried to have their jeans as dirty and worn as the bikers.

There were some who were not into the booze, drugs, and sex. They did not dress or talk or behave like the others. They never gave any impression that they had sex on their minds. They were usually wives or close girlfriends. They were often quiet and just wanted the chance to be out for a ride. But most of the women who hung out with the bikers fit the image of having been around the block a few times.

Mustang, one of the mamas from the Indiana chapter of the Iron Horsemen, climbed up on a pool table in a biker bar on Columbia Parkway and announced, "Everybody gather 'round, cause I am going to get my wings off the preacher right here and now. You ladies been talkin' about it, but I'm gonna get 'er done." Everyone applauded and yelled and laughed. They all looked at me for my response. She wore Horsemen colors which said, "Property of Dog."

I was surprised and embarrassed and didn't know what to say. Everybody got real quiet. I blurted out that I thought it was about time for her and Dog to get married. In spite of her having too much beer, she was sensitive to my embarrassment. One of the most rewarding experiences I had in my entire ministry with the gangs was when Mustang got down from the pool table, leaned over, and whispered, "I didn't mean to embarrass you. I am sorry for what I said." Every time I saw Mustang at a wedding or funeral, she came up to me to tell me how much she appreciated the service and the comments I made.

Packy put me through a test in front of some of the Horsemen when he asked, "What do you think about me and Sue shackin' up, me bein' married with two kids and all?" Sue was the teenaged daughter of a high-ranking city official.

It was very surprising to me to find out that several of the mamas, and some young girlfriends like Sue, were daughters, nieces, or some other relative of a court or city official. It was common in the late 60s and early 70s for rebellious, anti-establishment, drug-wise, street-hippy-type teenaged girls to reject the rigidity and middle-class lifestyle of their parents. The bikers with their long hair, beards, and individualism were perfect symbols of rebellion for these young women to latch on to.

I hesitated to make any response to Packy's question. He and the other Horsemen began to stare at me with looks that were confrontational and threatening. My blue suit and clerical collar didn't keep them from putting the squeeze on me. I think Packy thought it was time for a showdown. For weeks he had been trash-talking to me. He kept referring to Sue and how she wanted to wear his colors and be his property. When I would ride with them, he would always whiz by me and cut in front of me and laugh and give me the finger.

When I first began my contact with the Horsemen, I made it a point to let them know where I stood on the many questions of morality they threw at me. They needed to know how strongly I felt about what was right and wrong on the issues they brought up. So, in spite of Packy's previous intimidating behavior toward me, I jumped in with both feet.

"I think it is pretty sick! I think she is a fool for getting involved with you because you are just using her." Sue was sitting next to Packy. "You certainly aren't man enough to assume your responsibility as a husband and father and I think what you are doing is grossly irresponsible and immature."

When they pushed me with such confrontational nonsense, I usually got angry. I often said more than I should. And, it never sounded like it should come from the mouth of a preacher. (Especially when I was wearing my collar.) "You want to know what I *really* think?" (Whenever I raised that question it was strictly hypothetical. I never intended it as a question to be answered. Each time it came out of my mouth I immediately knew I had gone too far, that I had overstepped my boundaries, that I had passed the safe zone, and that I was heading for trouble.) What you are doing is plain chickenshit."

He looked at the other Horsemen and they just sat there listening. It was if they were thinking, *Ok, Packy, what are you going to do about this?* Sue got up from the couch to get a beer as if she was trying to break the tension and her own nervousness.

I had already gone too far, and figuring I didn't have much else to lose, I pushed it further by saying, "Thugs like you don't think of anyone but yourself. You want to keep having your own selfish way and taking advantage of people. You only cause problems and hurt for other people, especially your families. Think of Sue's family. They don't even know where she is. They probably are worried sick. You don't care. What about your wife and kids? When was the last time you saw them? I have no respect for people like you and I know you and Sue don't have respect or love for each other."

Instead of jumping up to punch me, or telling me to leave, he wanted to defend himself. "You're full of shit, man. Me and Sue dig each other. I don't dig my wife and she don't want me around. She left me. She is filing for divorce. Me and Sue are going to get married. And not by you, you asshole. So don't give me any more of your righteous mouth."

The other Horsemen just sat there. I wasn't going to push my luck any more. I got up to leave and looked at Sue who was standing behind the other Horsemen on

the couch. I tried to convey the question, "Can I take you home?" She seemed content to stay. I left.

When I was with a biker club, they would put me through a collective test. It was if they were all spectators to some challenge or dare they had for me. One time, when I first became acquainted with the Brothers In Arms, they were all gathered in the front yard of the parsonage with their bikes parked in the drive and in front of the church. They had come for a visit. But, the visit had a purpose. It was not to get acquainted, but to put me through a test. They were still trying to see what made the preacher tick. They were still trying to find out if I was someone they could trust. They wanted to know if their judgment of me from the shoulders down was real.

Sarge asked, "Preacher, have you ever done a wheelie?" They knew I did not have a street bike yet. They knew I raced, but they did not know if I had any experience doing a wheelie. I had done wheelies when I raced, I did them when I practiced on the track, and I did them to showboat in front of a crowd of spectators. Often, after a race was completed, some of the racers, especially the winner, would do a wheelie in front of the spectators as a grand finale. But I didn't tell them I could do a wheelie.

Several of them offered me their bike to use to do a wheelie down Chase Avenue in front of them as they gathered together in front of the church. They felt safe in the offer since they figured I would not take them up on their dare. After I picked out a bike from the many offered, I asked questions about how to do a wheelie. They each had a coaching technique for me which was given with a smile on their faces as if to say, "This is going to be a crash and burn spectacular. We are going to see what the preacher is really made of. He will never pull it off."

I rode down Chase Avenue and turned around in front of Chase School and rode toward them. I pulled off a wheelie right in front of them. They all yelled and waved as if they had witnessed one of their own meeting a challenge or dare. Days after, I thought, *Skipworth, you are really stupid. That stunt could have been a complete disaster. Doing a wheelie on a Harley Sportster is not an easy thing to do.* But, it drew me closer to the BIA.

Individual bikers would also test me on how I would react to the challenge of a fight. Too many times I heard, "I am going to see what the preacher is made of." In most cases the guy was stoned on drugs or drunk. Whenever it happened, I became more angry than afraid. I usually had my hose with me, but there was always another biker nearby who would look out for me. It was very comforting in those circumstances to know that there were guys who made sure no one messed with me.

One time, I was with the Horsemen on a river bank of the Great Miami River near Miamitown. A Horseman from the Hamilton chapter challenged me to a fight. He said, "I've heard about you, preacher. I want to find out what you are made of." I had my hose with me and this time I had the cotton saturated with kerosene, rubbing alcohol, and Mogan David wine. He didn't know about the hose that I carried. When I pulled it out of the back of the jacket, he looked at it like it was a bazooka. He stopped walking toward me and just looked me in the eye. Several Horsemen from the Cincinnati chapter came over and stood between us. Big Dave told him "If you don't want that hose wrapped around your head, you better back off. The preacher can take care of himself, but we are here to make sure nobody messes with the preacher."

There were only a few guys that challenged me like that, and most of them had too many beers. I learned who I could trust and who to stay away from.

I had a few calls from parents asking me to see if I could locate a son or daughter who had been missing for a few days. A father from Mt. Healthy called and told me that his son had been missing for two days. He said he may be hanging out with one of the outlaw biker clubs in the Clifton area. He described his son to me, gave me his name, and asked if I would be on the lookout for him.

Usually, high school kids who were runaways found themselves in Clifton at either the Reflections or the Black Dome. Those are the places where the crowds gather and bikers always seem to be there. On this particular night, I thought it best if I wore my blue suit and collar. I was going to make some inquiries and wanted to come off as pastoral. I didn't have my hose. I never found a way to attach it to the back of my blue suit.

One biker, from a club I had never heard of before, stood near the entrance of the Black Dome in Clifton. He kept looking and listening to me while I was talking to some of the bystanders and musicians. I guess my questions were too probing for him. Maybe it was just another test I was being put through. It was as if I was intruding in his territory and business. All of a sudden he took his beer bottle, held it by its neck and busted it against a brick wall, and started walking toward me. He was about my size and build but I was sure I was in better shape. Besides, he was half-drunk.

Nevertheless, I never took chances with those guys who had too much liquor. As soon as this one got within arms-length, I pushed him against the front doors of the Black Dome and stood face to face with him. He never blinked. He grabbed me by the throat with one hand and I held his arm with the broken bottle. He stuck part of the jagged edge into the sleeve of my suit coat and cut my wrist. Two or three women, maybe mamas from his club, grabbed him by his hair and got him off me. They all went into the Dome. I didn't follow. I gave up my search for the young man from Mt. Healthy that night.

One of the worst tests I went through was in the basement in the home of one of the Horsemen. Some Renegades were there. One of them and his mama just stared at me with a glassy-eyed, silly grin. He was sitting backward in a chair with an American flag draped over his shoulders. His mama was sitting next to him. I was at a table right next to theirs. After a while, he pulled a gun and pointed it at me. He and his mama continued staring at me with their silly grins. He had been sitting in that position most of the evening, drinking beer. He never talked to anyone the whole evening. They both just stared at me. Not many people saw what was happening. The noise, the music, and everything else kept on going.

After a few seconds (it seemed like a long time to me) he put down the gun and those who noticed laughed at the joke. I stared back at him and kicked the back of his chair and knocked him backward out of the chair. Lucky for me, we were in the home of one of the Horsemen and they seldom put me through tests like that and they didn't like it when someone else did. Richie and Toad went over and took the gun and told him and his mama to leave. I made it a point never to be around the Renegades again. Especially him; he was like a loose cannon.

Other tests they put me through included offering me pills to see if I would take them, asking me to hide a runaway teenaged girlfriend, lying for them in court, to their wives, or to loan companies. They wanted to know if I would keep stolen goods at the parsonage. Once, they wanted me to open the church so they could have a party. They wanted me to make a job recommendation for them when they knew I knew they would not keep the job. These were all tests and they knew my responses before they confronted me. What was interesting was that the Brothers In Arms, the Henchmen, and the Iron Horsemen seldom tested me or allowed anyone else to test me. When I was with them, they made sure "no one messes with the preacher."

I wasn't sure how the clubs or individual bikers would take it when they found out I was being invited to speak at churches, schools, and other groups about my ministry to them. This could have been another problem. I asked several bikers to come to the house to talk about it. Seven different clubs were represented. I told them that since the article appeared in the *Cincinnati Post and Times Star* about my ministry to them, I had been invited to several churches, schools, and other groups to speak about them and my involvement with them. "I don't want to get myself in trouble with you over this. I don't want you to hear about it from someone besides me and not hear the truth about what I have said. I am not asking for your permission. I am asking you to trust me."

Filthy Phil said, "You call it like you see it. If you ever want one of us or all of us to go with you, we will be glad to. Don't think you have to make us out as boy scouts." Round sent Farmer John to the meeting and he summed it up very well. "You can't say anything about us that the newspapers and television stations haven't already. You sure as hell won't make it that bad. When you go speak to these people, wear your collar. Look like a preacher. Tell them you're our preacher."

I was asked to speak at one of the junior high schools of one of the suburban school systems. The teacher asked the students to write their responses to my presentation. The following are some of their comments:

—Everyone here thinks that Reverend Skipworth is doing good because he is helping people who need help the most. If the church can't help them, who can? Or, will?

—We think that many people shouldn't go out and do this work, if a whole bunch went out to do this, the gangs would rebel against it.

—Reverend Skipworth really cares about them and he shows it. He doesn't stop even if he gets beat up, he just keeps going until he reaches them. He sacrifices his time and even his life, helping those gangs.

—One thing that impressed all of us, was that he made the decision to do this himself. He didn't have to and he wasn't forced. Also, he knows he is right and doesn't care what people think.

—Everybody thought he was a real good guy. He risked getting beat up by the gangs, cause he felt it is important to reach those guys in the motorcycle gangs. The way he preaches is really good, too, because he does not force them to listen, they can if they want to. He didn't talk to us like a preacher either.

—We didn't think a priest could make friends with a motorcycle gang. He associates with different types of people like God did.

—He stayed with those people even though they beat him up.

—If he changes them a little, it's better than none.

—The gangs could have thrown a knife in his back anytime, but instead they just beat him up.

—He must have been pretty good because they trusted him. When that guy shot that girl, he came to Reverend Skipworth because he trusted him.

—We think Skippy is a real smooth guy. He spreads the word kind of good. He takes a lot of chances because it is kind of dangerous with those kinds of guys. He was doing kind of the same thing Jesus was doing.

—We thought Skip was good because he talked about real problems. He talked about why they should join the church. He didn't really care what they looked like as long as he got people in the church. He understands them because he works with them. Maybe some of them were scared of God and left God. Skip brought them back.

—We think his cause is worthwhile. We like the stuff he is doing to help these people. We feel he is doing the right thing and we think he is doing it the right way.

—We think he's like a modern day Jesus. He's trying to teach these people about God who don't want to learn. We'd like to have him come back so we could learn more about his work. We think he is a good leader, but he needs more followers.

—People talk about taking care of this stuff, but they don't do anything. Reverend Skipworth is one of the people who's getting involved.

—He is a great guy because he doesn't care what people think of him just as long as he knows he's doing the right thing. And he is.

There were thirty students in the class and they were divided into five different discussion groups to discuss and write down their comments. The teacher sent me their comments and I filed them in my scrapbook. I shared the comments from the students with several different bikers. When they read the comments about me being beaten, some were quick to point out, "I hope to hell you didn't tell them it was us who beat you up." They also said, "I am glad you didn't call us any bad names."

Another potential problem I could see for myself was that when I was riding with a particular club and was identified as one of them while they were at war with another club. When we would pull up next to the opposing club, that club never said, "Hello, Rev. Skipworth, glad to see you. You better ride on home now." They never acknowledged my presence as a minister. They hardly even looked at me. They just talked about what would happen if we didn't get our "shit together." I knew it would be stupid to say something like, "Well, remember guys, I am really a minister and it's not my role to fight with these guys, so leave me out of this hassle. I just happen to be riding with them right now."

When these situations occurred I tried to play the role of reconciler/peacemaker by inviting the two gang leaders to come to the house to talk it over. Sometimes it worked. When I found that nothing I said was going to work, I excused myself and left. I got tired of those encounters and I told them more than once, "This is nothing more than immature junior high nonsense."

They reacted to this by saying, "This ain't play, preacher. This is takin' no shit from nobody. Go home."

It was always a problem when a club lost sight of my role with them. Sometimes they started expecting more of me than just an advisor or middle man. At two o'clock one morning, I received a phone call from the Cobras asking me to meet them immediately and to wear my collar. I had just gotten home from Christ Hospital where I had been with a family from the church.

I met the Cobras, thinking it might be some kind of emergency. When I rode my bike to meet them at the designated spot, they told me they were going to the Broken Drum, the meeting place of the Devil's Disciples. They told me, "They roughed up Birdman and we need to hear what they got to say about it.

I asked them, "Why did you call me? Why did you want me to ride my bike over here? What do you want me to do? Why did you want me to wear my collar?" While I was waiting for an answer, they took off.

Like a fool, I followed. I had no idea what I was going to do when we got there. Fortunately, nothing happened since there were sixteen Cobras and only two Devil's Disciples. With those kinds of odds, even bikers can negotiate. As we got on our bikes to leave, I told the Cobras, "Don't ever do this again. If you want to get it on with someone, invite them to come to the house and we will talk it over. But, don't ever drag me into something like this again. What the hell did you think I was going to do? Birdman, you follow me home. You are going to pay the babysitter and you are going to explain to her mother what the hell is going on."

One of my colleagues who was serving a United Methodist Church in Hamilton called and asked me for some help. He told me that the parents of a sixteen-year-old girl in his church came to see him and told him that their daughter ran off with a member of the Iron Horsemen of the Hamilton chapter. He told me he called the

police and the police asked him to call me to see if I could get her away from the IH. He said the police did not want to risk getting into a confrontation with the IH because someone might get hurt. "Can you help us, Skip?"

I never expected this kind of problem, either. I told him I would see what I could do. He said the police would give me twenty-four hours.

I called Crazy Horse, told him my problem, and asked if he would go with me to the Hamilton chapter of the Horsemen to help me get the girl.

He told me, "Horsemen of one chapter don't get involved with the business of another chapter. What goes on up there is none of our business. I can't help you out. Tell your preacher friend to keep his ass out of it. And, you keep your ass out of it, too." He hung up.

I called him back. I asked, "Would you at least go with me? I don't even know where their chapter house is."

"Preacher, I told you to keep your ass out of this. I am not going to go up there." He hung up again.

I called him back again. "I am going to get the girl out of there. I will just have to find the place on my own. I am going to do it whether you help me or not. What are you afraid of? They are your brothers."

"I am not afraid of anything, you stupid prick. You go up there and you will get yourself stomped. You are the stupidest asshole I have ever met. Leave me alone." I could hear him cursing me as he slammed down the phone.

As I sat in my office thinking of my next move, Crazy Horse called. He was loud and sounded frustrated and angry. "OK, I will take you up there, but I am going to drop you off at the end of the lane that goes to their house. You will be on your own. I am only going to give you thirty minutes to get the job done. I'll wait for you where I drop you off. But, I am warning you, they are really going to be pissed. They won't give that girl up to anybody. You don't have shit for brains. You are going to have to be carried back to the car." I thought Crazy Horse was beginning to mellow.

It was late at night and very cold when he picked me up and drove to the meeting house. As he said he would, he dropped me off at the end of the lane going up to the meeting house. I got out and started walking up the dark tree-lined lane to an old farmhouse. Crazy Horse got out of the car and slammed the door. "Preacher, you are the most ignorant bastard I know. Get back in the car and I will take you up there." Crazy Horse kept calling me names and letting me know how stupid I was. Now, I knew he was softening up.

After a walk of about forty or fifty yards we were standing on the front porch. As I started to knock, Crazy Horse pushed my arm away, opened the door and we walked in. Under his breath he said to me, "You got me in one fuckin' mess." Everybody seemed shocked to see us standing there. Here was Crazy Horse, one of their brothers, with a preacher in a blue suit and clerical collar under an overcoat.

Nobody knew why we were there. There were other women there, but it didn't take long to identify the young girl named Rachel, the girl we came for. She was standing next to a guy who was short and dumpy and twice her age. I walked over to her, stood in front of her and told her, "Your parents are very concerned about you and asked if I would come and get you and take you home."

The president of the chapter said, "She ain't goin' nowhere. Who the fuck are you?"

Crazy Horse told him, "This is the preacher. He rides with us."

The president told me, "You get your ass out of here. We don't want no preacher around here."

Another member of the Hamilton chapter was standing in the doorway of another room. He heard all that was going on and said to the president and the others, while looking at me, "I seen the preacher before." Then he spoke to me. "What do you have to do with this girl?"

"I am a friend of her pastor. He asked me on behalf of her parents to come and get her. Otherwise, in less than twenty-four hours the police will be here and someone will get hurt. I guarantee you, all the Iron Horsemen of Hamilton will be locked up if I don't take Rachel to her parents. Let's go Rachel."

She came over to us as if she was glad we had come. She grabbed her coat off a chair. Nobody said a word. Nobody made a move toward us. Crazy Horse, Rachel, and I left immediately. As we walked hurriedly to the car, Crazy Horse said, "Preacher, you got balls."

Crazy Horse drove us to her home. I waited for Crazy Horse to walk up to the door with me. He said he had had enough for one evening. Rachel's minister, my colleague, was waiting with the parents and Rachel's older sister. I didn't stay for conversation or explanation. I received a wonderful letter of thanks from the parents which I shared with Crazy Horse. After he read their words of thanks, he began to see what a wonderful deed he had done.

Becoming involved with the narcotics agent whom I mentioned earlier was another potential problem I never anticipated. In spite of the hardcore image of an undercover cop, he had a compassionate nature about him and he often asked me

to add one more person to my list of outcasts. It was as if he was in charge of a church prayer chain and would add persons needing prayer. After the bust was made in Clifton, Greenie asked me to help with a seventeen-year-old juvenile who used to hang out with the Brothers In Arms. He wanted me to appear with the kid when he went for his hearing. His name was Wally. He had done some minor deals with drugs and could have been on his way to serving some serious prison time. Greenie would also be there at Wally's hearing.

I stood in the hall in the court house with Wally and his mother. Greenie had not yet arrived. Wally didn't know he was coming or that he was the narc responsible for the drug bust. When Greenie walked up to us, his hair was cut, he had shaved his beard, he was wearing a suit and tie, and he was carrying a briefcase. I had a hard time recognizing him as the no-good drug pusher I met at the chili parlor just weeks ago.

"Hi, Wally." Greenie held out his hand to shake Wally's hand.

"Whose this dude, man? I don't need no lawyer, I got one. How do you know my name, man?

"I'm Greenie, from the street." Wally showed a smile of surprise.

"Hey, man, you got busted, too? You got all cleaned up. You tryin' to impress the judge? Hey, preacher, look at this jag." Wally started laughing.

Greenie pulled out his badge and Wally started cursing and took a swing at him. I held him back and Greenie said to him, "On the street you always talked big about doing your own thing and that everybody should do theirs. Well, I was doing mine. Now, the preacher and I are here to help you today. We don't want you to go to prison. I think we can work it out. You have too much on the ball and I don't want to see you get wasted."

After Wally cooled down, he shook Greenie's hand and began to cry. He was scared. He kept saying, "This ain't for real, man. I'm dreamin; Greenie is a narc."

With the evidence presented in Wally's case and Greenie's testimony, he received a short sentence of four months in the Hamilton Juvenile Detention Center. While at the center, he had his eighteenth birthday. When he was released, he joined the army and was eventually sent to Vietnam, where he was killed. Wally was one of four funerals I had of Vietnam vets.

After the drug bust that he and his partner put together, Greenie was never on the street again. I never had much contact with him when he worked Clifton since it might jeopardize his work. After all, many of the bikers were going to go down with the bust. The only private talk I had with him was in my car, parked in a dark alley near Reflections, when he showed me how to make the weapon from the hose. He was very concerned about my safety and kept saying not to take any chances.

When he dropped from the scene, he called me on occasion just to keep in touch. I received a call from him one day inviting me to his home in Anderson Township. I had a pleasant visit with him, his wife, and two daughters over dinner.

While I was visiting him, he gave me a copy of the following letter which was written to his boss, the attorney general of the State of Ohio. The letter was from a man in Cleveland who had heard me speak at his church. The letter was sent to the attorney general to call his attention to my ministry to the gangs. When Greenie gave me the copy of the letter, I understood why he took such an interest in me and was concerned for my safety.

November 7, 1969

Mr. Paul Brown
Attorney General
State House
Columbus, Ohio

Dear Mr. Brown:

Enjoyed meeting you and hearing you speak at the Ohio Association of Life Underwriters Association Convention in October.

As you recall, I tried to speak with you a couple of times and we finally agreed that I would write you a letter explaining what's on my mind.

There's a young Methodist minister in Cincinnati you should know about. His name is Rev. Gene Skipworth and he's pastor of the Northside Methodist Church on Chase and Delaney. What makes him worthy of notice by your office, I feel, is that he rides a motorcycle, provided by his church, with a motorcycle gang, which is, by anyone's definition, a tough bunch.

I met Gene at a retreat not long ago and was impressed by his courage, his attitude and his dedication. He is working, as I understand it, with the cooperation of the Cincinnati police. He has cooperated with some narcotics agents in the past—perhaps even from your office.

He is associating with these youths in their world. He accepts them as they are as a start. This enables him to be with them, perhaps as a father would, when crises arise. It's at these critical times when they seek, and are influenced by, his advice. He has prevented many "rumbles" with rival gangs and is hard at work to guide all the gangs toward more peaceful activities. Gene has the respect of these young men, to a large degree, because he enters into organized motorcycle racing events. They turn out to watch him, although they, themselves, do not participate.

To almost any casual observer, these gang members appear as obvious "hoods" or "punks." Probably if Gene were not interested in helping them they would become one more drop in the vast cesspool of human misfits and castoffs. Certainly there is no guarantee that he can rehabilitate them. Indeed, in the end, they may destroy him.

Sensing all this, I began to open as many doors for him as possible through my business and church contacts in Cincinnati. Gene was too "far out" for most people at the outset of his efforts. He wears a beard (not a shaggy one I'm happy to say) to show the gang members that he accepts them and some of their mores. Meantime things are looking up, but at a painfully slow pace. Gene's racing activities are costing more than he or his church can afford. One smash-up and he's in trouble, to say nothing of the physical hazards. Several of the local cycle shops are "carrying" him temporarily, but in the end, everyone must be paid.

Certainly I'm not suggesting that your office offer financial assistance. I am suggesting that his mission might be considered important enough to warrant some kind attention and moral support from your office, which in turn, may very well hasten the support of some of the city fathers in Cincinnati. Some, who are sympathetic, are holding back until they feel Gene has a 100% Good Housekeeping Seal of approval. Meantime, Gene may or may not survive alone. He is considering leaving the ministry to give his full time and effort to re-directing these youths.

At first, my feeling was simply that this was Cincinnati's problem and that I had my hands full with community involvement in Cleveland. But I cannot get Gene off my mind. That's why I responded to the concern and sensitivity I heard coming from you in your impassioned comments in Columbus.

May I ask that you give Gene's cause some consideration? His influence could, with help from the right sources, spread to other Ohio cities. My concern is that he gets help before either his cause dies or he does.

Thanks for listening. If I can be of any further assistance to you, please let me know.

Respectfully,

H. L. Akin
Vice President, Empire Life Insurance Company of Ohio
717 Superior Avenue N.E.
Cleveland, Ohio 44114

After I read the letter from Mr. Akin, I understood why Greenie and his partner took such an interest in me and my ministry. Their boss, the attorney general of the state of Ohio, obviously passed the letter from Mr. Akin to them and told them to watch my back. If not for the letter from Mr. Akin, I may not have survived being on the streets with the gangs. Greenie did watch my back, he helped me fashion "the hose," he taught me how to use it, and he let me know who the crazies to watch out for were. It was about two years after the letter was written when Greenie showed it to me. The longer I considered Mr. Akin's gesture, the more I thought he saved my life.

Mr. Akin invited me to his church in Hudson, Ohio to speak and he enabled me to tell my story to many other audiences such as business groups, schools, and civic organizations.

Mr. Akin embraced me and my ministry due to his own Christian convictions dealing with missions and evangelism. The letter he wrote to the attorney general was not only insurance for my well-being at that time, but proved how much he was committed to sharing in my work. In those two years of our communicating back and forth to each other, he never mentioned the letter he had written.

CHAPTER NINE

The most enjoyable times I had with the bikers were when one of the clubs would invite me, my kids, and three or four other clubs over to one of their houses for a cookout. These were times when the families of the bikers gathered with their kids, wives, and girlfriends. Seldom did fights break out. No one had to prove how tough they were. No one needed to gross anybody out to impress or maintain an image. Kids were present and it seemed that everyone was there just to have a good time. Everyone was on good behavior and considerate of others. The neighbors were often invited, which meant that there were some non-bikers present. Those club members who had backyards usually served as hosts.

The cookouts were some of the few times I felt I really could minister one-on-one with the families of the biker clubs. At the first one I attended, I was surprised to be asked to offer a blessing. Each time we were invited to a cookout, I was asked to pray before we ate. Before I prayed, I asked if anyone knew of someone in their family or friends who needed prayer or a visit from me. During the time of the cookout, I would visit around with everyone there. I was always made to feel welcome. Those were rare gatherings when the bikers and their families were like everybody else. Their marriages seemed like ordinary marriages. But, in the ongoing everyday lifestyle of the biker subculture, that was far from reality.

On one particular Sunday we were invited to one of those afternoon cookouts. We took along our dish to pass. Almost everyone came in cars, but some bikers came with their wives or girlfriends on back of the bike, cradling their dish to pass. A biker cookout was not the same as a church picnic/cookout. The dress code was different. We had soft drinks available, but beer was usually cooled in several large tubs filled with ice. The conversations were never centered around church and what was going on at the church. The church budget was not an issue to be discussed. They never used church tables and chairs; they didn't have access to them. I offered them use of the NUMC tables and chairs but they never took me up on it. People brought card tables and their own chairs. Usually, I was the only one related to a church.

The menu was not extensive. The host used his grill with charcoal and lighter fluid. Hamburgers and hotdogs were the main items on the menu. I never knew which wife or girlfriend was noted for special dishes. At church picnics and cook-outs one could expect Mrs. Kagy to have her specialty, fried chicken; Mrs. Brannock would bring her potato salad; Mrs. Bonecutter, her baked beans. At church picnics we anticipated who was going to bring what and looked forward to those special dishes. Nevertheless, at the biker cookouts, we had plenty of great food to eat.

But at this particular cookout, at the home of one of the nicest and most gentle of all the bikers, things got out of control. Grease was the host and a member of the Nomads and spent a lot of time at our home. Never did he act in such a way that I felt he had to be reined in. He had my kids over to his home to play with his son. His wife was one of the most devoted mothers and wives of any of the bikers. We looked forward to being at his home for the cookout.

The Prophets, Satan's Sinners, and Fugeros also were there. Things were going very well until Pearl, a member of the Fugeros, started yelling at his wife and pushing her around. I was standing near them with a plate full of food. His wife had their little boy in her arms as he began hitting her. She turned away from him and his fists to protect the little boy. It was obvious he had too much to drink. He really was beginning to lose control. He was punching her in the head and back and all the time she was trying to protect the baby. Grease, who was busy grilling the burgers and dogs, yelled at Walt, one of the Fugeros, who was nearby, to stop him. Everybody was watching in disbelief. A beautiful afternoon was quickly getting ruined.

When he reared his arm to hit his wife again, I handed my plate to someone and got him in a stranglehold and threw him to the ground. He was fighting to get up and kept yelling and cursing his wife. I looked up to see where she was and could see the alarm and fear in her eyes and heard the screams of the little boy. I began to get to the point where an adrenaline rush was taking place in me instead of being cool. I was straddled on top of him and I wanted to use my fists on him. Then I realized I had a fork in my right hand. I had it up against his cheek near his eye. When

he rolled his eyes toward it and felt it against his skin, he stopped struggling. I suddenly realized what I was doing. I threw the fork away and got up.

Walt and some of his brothers were standing over us. They held him down and tried to cool him off. The cookout was over. His wife didn't seem to be hurt but she was very upset and embarrassed. Grease's wife and several other women attended to her and the baby. A few days later, she moved to her parents' home in Dayton. I don't remember any of the Fugeros being invited to another cookout. I don't remember ever going to another cookout. I don't remember seeing Pearl again or his wife.

That was the first case of spousal abuse or domestic violence I had ever witnessed. But as I rode with the bikers I became aware of other instances of a wife or girlfriend being beaten by her man. For some reason, I thought I would encounter it more often among the outlaw bikers. That was not a fair judgment to make of them. Every segment of society is guilty of domestic violence. From the rich to the poor, the educated to the dropout, the religious to the non-religious. It occurs in all types of families and in all religions throughout the world. But, because of the violent nature of the bikers, the role of tough guy they always played, and because they seldom exhibited any sign of thoughtfulness or consideration toward their women, I expected to encounter more wife or girlfriend abuse. This expectation was enhanced when I saw how the women were caught up in the role the woman played as being property of the biker. Each woman wore colors that stated she was the property of someone.

In the late 60s and early 70s, with the feminist movement coming into fruition, the concept and idea of women being property was beginning to lose its appeal. But, certainly not among bikers and their women. There was no question which woman belonged to whom, what her expectations and roles were, and what her status was within the sub-culture of the biker world.

Until the early part of the twentieth century, husbands were instructed by law to beat their wives with a stick no greater than the thickness of their thumb; thus the coining of the phrase "rule of thumb."

In 1895, some states began adopting the Married Women's Property Act, which gave women some rights to own property and made the husband's conviction for assault sufficient grounds for divorce. This act signifies the beginning of a shift away from the concept that women were their husbands' property. Within the world and mindset of the biker, this law did not apply. His treatment of "his woman" was nobody's business but his own. This fit the findings of a poll taken in 1970 that found that one out of five Americans, women included, approved a man hitting his wife in certain circumstances.

I knew only of three other cases of domestic violence within the biker clubs. Such an issue was not discussed. Bikers did not talk much about the family, what the family did, vacations, backgrounds, and their own personal upbringing. What took place in their homes was very private. I would often inquire about their families and homes. The comment I most often received was, "None of your fuckin' business, preacher," or, a short three-word sentence like "Things are OK," or no comment at all.

The phrase "domestic violence" was not on the front burner of the American family scene in the late 60s and early 70s. The first shelter for battered women, Haven House, in San Gabriel, California, did not open its doors until 1964. Even in that time of the liberation movement among women, the biker woman rarely sought help or could find a way out. First, there was no place for them to go and no one to talk to. In 1975, the National Organization for Women (NOW) formed a task force on battered women. In 1978, the National Coalition Against Domestic Violence was organized to establish grassroots shelters and service programs around the nation.

Among the bikers, the issue of domestic violence was hidden easily from outside the home. The battered wife or girlfriend became a recluse. Her self-esteem and confidence often collapsed due to the emotional, physical, and verbal abuse. Living with an abusive mate left her feeling depressed, despondent, and defeated. Friends, relatives, and neighbors would find it hard to believe that her husband, even if he was an outlaw biker, could do such a thing as beat her. She received very little empathy from her fellow biker mamas and old ladies.

In those days, and even today, talking to their minister, if they had one, could be risky. Snake's wife had a minister. When she called me and told me that Snake had raped and beaten her and insisted she be a train for some of his brothers, she asked in great desperation, "What can I do?" I told her to talk to her minister and see if he knew of someone who could take her in for a while. She said she had talked to him and he told her to perform her duty to Snake and be a more obedient wife.

There was no place, no shelter for these women and their children to go. I took in bikers who had dropped out of their club to protect them from their brothers who were seeking revenge. It would have been wonderful if I could have used the parsonage as a shelter for battered women, but the husbands and their brothers

would have stormed the parsonage to get them back. Having a biker stay at the parsonage after they dropped out was not as risky. They could take care of themselves, they didn't stay very long, it cost me no money, they were capable of going off on their own when things cooled down, they had no kids with them, and there were no legal or social implications. But, to provide a safe haven for abused wives and children would have been too risky and probably impossible. There would have been great risk to our home and church property if a crazed husband or boyfriend and his fellow bikers came storming into the house to retrieve his woman. There would have been the risk of harm to the woman and her children and risk to me and my children. Confidentiality would not have been possible and it would have been impossible financially. The risks were too great and I was not trained to handle such a complex social issue.

Another reason the biker woman could not find a solution to her problem was that she was immersed in the role of being property or possession of a biker. It was just her lot in life; this was the way it was supposed to be. Her role was further defined by the biker club her husband or boyfriend belonged to. The wife or girlfriend not only knew her role with her guy, she also knew she was in a subservient role to the gang as well. Leaving the guy was also leaving the club he belonged to. It was a case of having more than one guy to fear.

There were other ways the biker would control his wife or girlfriend besides physical abuse. There was the emotional abuse that the spouse had to go through. This was common with the name-calling, the minor battering incidents such as pushing, shoving, and throwing food. There were threats that he would take the children away, kill the family pet, or destroy a particularly important heirloom or memento of his wife like Red did with his wife's flute.

Many of the bikers wanted to control their wives. Pud, a member of the Henchmen, was one of the most Archie Bunker types I had encountered. His father treated his mother in a very domineering way and that was the way he was going to treat Alma. Alma was supposed to take care of all his needs. She was to be there whenever and wherever he wanted. She was to have a meal ready and on the table whenever he wanted. He would not let her drive and would not let her get a job. He wanted her at home all the time. She had no life of her own. He took care of what little money they had, and would not give her an allowance to use for the kids or the household needs. She never knew how much money they had or where it was. Pud was a total control freak.

Alma called and asked me, if Pud would agree to it, could they come and see me. She said, "We were married in my church, the Roman Catholic Church. He agreed to be married there and he agreed to raise our kids Roman Catholic. He was such a nice guy then. I didn't know he was like his father, and I didn't think he would try to dominate me like he does. I know he will not go see my priest, but he may be willing to come to see you. It's all because of those biker friends of his."

I didn't think there was much chance of her getting him to come and see me. But she did. I was always curious as to why he came, but I was not going to press the issue. They came and brought their two-year-old daughter with them.

Something was going on inside Pud when they came in the house. He was very mellow, kind, thoughtful, especially to Alma. He held their little girl. We sat down in my office. I asked if they would mind if I prayed. Alma nodded yes and Pud said, "That would be good."

Alma surprised me. For a wife who was so dominated and seemed to be a doormat for this overbearing macho gang member, she laid it out very clearly. "Dave (Pud's real name) won't let me drive the car. He says I can't work but we need the money. All I do is stay at home with the baby and take orders from him. He has all his friends. I have none. He tells his parents to stay out of our lives and he won't let me visit my mother. I feel so alone. I have no one. And I don't know what to do."

"Pud, did you hear all that Alma said?"

"Yeah."

"What do you have to say about it all?"

"I came with her today, didn't I?" There was a long pause. I didn't say anything and neither did Alma. Pud fingered his little daughter's hair. Then he said, very unexpectedly, "I need you to help me get out of the Henchmen. They plan to go to war with the Horsemen. I don't want any part of it."

"So, you only came here with Alma because you want out of the Henchmen?" I was getting ready to ask another question about Alma and the baby, but he interrupted me and said, "I am here because of Alma and the baby. I want us to have a proper family. I don't want the stuff with the Henchmen. I want to get back to my job and family."

This session was one of the few that turned out successfully. Alma and Pud made it happen. In most cases, there would be no counseling session with a couple, and when it did happen, and questions were raised, the guy usually stomped out.

I played peacemaker between Pud and his fellow Henchmen. It was one of the few times I was successful in that role. I called Pud and Alma a couple of times after

our conversation at the office. The next time I saw them was when I visited Alma at the hospital when she had their second child.

Most of the wives of the bikers had an impossible role to play. Many of them made the excuse that her husband was in a biker club because it was a stage he is going through. One of the wives of the Devil's Disciples called me and told me she was having all kinds of problems with her parents because of her husband's involvement with the Devils. I asked her why she put up with her husband belonging with the Devils. She said, "Well, maybe it is just a stage he is going through." I am sure she said the same thing about her four-year-old son. She asked if I would talk to her husband. I told her I would try. I wasn't successful.

I made the mistake of asking him, "What does your wife think about your being a Devil's Disciple?"

"I don't give a shit what she thinks. My brothers come first." That was a common response from the bikers I talked to. In so many cases, the wife eventually had to give him an ultimatum in anger and frustration, "Either you leave that bunch of cycle-trash, or I leave you." Most often, the bikers chose their brothers.

Some wives went to great lengths to humor their husbands and go along with their participation in an outlaw biker club. The wife would let him dip into a sparse family budget to get an old Harley chopper that wouldn't run and needed all kinds of repairs and parts. She wore the colors which said, "Property of . . ." She watched him try to ride a Harley chopper for the first time and almost get killed. She watched him go through the humiliation of being a pledge, participating in all kinds of childish, embarrassing behavior. She saw him trying to impress his brothers with crazy stunts, heard him make all kinds of gross, out-of-character comments, and witnessed behavior that was completely foreign to what they knew about him. A very embarrassing and uncomfortable expectation was the demand that she call her husband by his nickname and not his real name. Wives referred to their husbands as "Demon," "Roach," "Scarface," and "Toad" instead of Jerry, Steve, David, and Gene.

The wife of a Nomad called me and told me that her husband had just called and told her to go out and buy several cases of beer because the club was coming over to the house. Her concern was not having a few of them over for drinking beer, but all the Nomads? She was concerned about her two kids. She also was very concerned about what her neighbors would think, how the house and yard would look after they left, how long the beer party would go on, and what would happen if the police were called. She said she told her husband she was concerned about all those bikes and bikers pulling up in the yard with all the noise, disturbance, and problems they might cause. She said he told her, "Just get the damn beer."

I made another mistake. I told her to take the kids and leave and I would go over to the house and talk to him and the Nomads. I got there before they arrived. When the Nomads arrived, they pulled their bikes in the yard, out in the street, and even in some of the neighbors' driveways. Bear's wife was right in her anticipation of potential problems. Bear was very surprised to see me waiting in his front yard with my car parked in his drive.

Right away he knew what was going on. "Did Norma call you?"

"Yes, she was concerned about you guys having a beer party here. She didn't want the neighbors upset. She didn't want the police to show up at the house. She was afraid and embarrassed. There is no beer here, Bear. You guys will have to go someplace else."

"Preacher, you mind your own fuckin' business and get your ass out of here."

One of the Nomads opened my car door and another pushed me in. I left.

Several neighbors saw it all and I am sure the police came soon after I left. The Nomads and I were never on speaking terms after that.

Wives put up with days lost from their husbands' work because they were out messing around with their brothers. The wives put up bail money they didn't have to get their husbands out of jail. The wife had to go through the confusing and agonizing experience of seeing her husband try to be something/someone he was not, of seeing an abrupt change in his behavior, and having him treat her and their children abusively. Many wives asked me, "What can I do about it?"

I found out that "I will talk to him about it" never worked. In each case the husband told me to mind my own business. They all said the same thing, "My brothers come first: before her, the kids, me, my family, and, preacher, God."

After all the hassles some of the wives went through for weeks and months, a few finally came to the point where they had had it. They said they were tired of his dirty friends, the way he treated them, and how he stopped assuming responsibility around the house and with the family. A few of them said they also got tired of the constant question from their mothers, "What's he trying to do to you and the kids?" After the ultimatum to him, if the wife was lucky, he would drop out of the gang.

One of the wives of the Iron Horsemen stood out to me. She was very nice, pretty, and petite. She was unique in that she was a college graduate, a Sunday

school teacher, church choir member, a Brownie troop leader, and she had a very good job. They were married only ten months when her husband joined and got actively involved with the Iron Horsemen. She thought his participation with the gang would run its course and he would realize it was not the place for him.

She was one of the few persons, so closely related to a biker club, who were involved with a church. That made her especially appreciative of all that I was trying to do. She was patient with her husband. Her pastor told her to let things go for awhile, pray, and hopefully her husband would drop out. Things kept getting worse as her husband got more involved. She never wanted to force her husband to make a choice between her and the Horsemen. But, she eventually did. As with most of the cases I dealt with, he chose the Horsemen and he and his wife were divorced.

CHAPTER TEN

I wonder what outlaw motorcycle club members would be like if they rode the streets today. I believe they would look just like they did from 1969 to 1972: long hair, beards, dirty jeans, boots, tattoos, worn and greasy colors. They would be identified easily because they would still wear the same uniform. Their Nazi insignias and helmets would fit in well with the skin heads prevalent today. Most of them would wear bandanas around their heads and under their helmets. They would still try to freak people out. They would still be out to do their own thing. They still would not take any crap from anybody. They would try to intimidate people and think nothing of terrorizing them.

I can't picture them having a cell phone case hanging from their sprocket chain-belt weapon. I doubt if they would be seen working with an iPod. I don't see them gathering at a Starbucks to sit down to have a conversation about a retaliation strike over a cappuccino with skim milk. Or plugging in their laptops at Panera's. I can't imagine them being involved as participants in a Parent Teachers Organization meeting and not wanting to run it. I don't think they would wear Old Navy or Abercrombie clothes. I don't think they would take in a night of bowling or join a golf league. I wonder what category of books I would see them browsing in at Barnes and Noble. I doubt if they would have leaf blowers in their garages sitting next to their Harley choppers. Sitting on a Toro mower would not be their way of "getting it on." A diet coke would not be on their diet. Joining a health club would be considered "fairy" to them. The only time they would use the word "recycle" would be to paraphrase Cutter's remark to a citizen who stepped in his way, "You want me to recycle you?"

There are very few one-percenter outlaw motorcycle clubs today like the Iron Horsemen, Devil's Disciples, and Brothers In Arms. Most motorcycle riders belong to a club that is American Motorcycle Association sanctioned. There are several biker clubs that are Christian related. Bikers for Jesus, Christ On Two Wheels, Riders With Jesus, are just a few. In the past ten to fifteen years, I have seen one-percenter clubs join in parades with the American flag flying from the back of the bike seat. None of the outlaw biker clubs I was familiar with would have joined in any of those parades. They certainly would not have flown the American flag from one of their bikes.

I am not sure why there are fewer outlaw bikers around today than were in existence when I rode with the outlaw bikers of the late 60s. I was in contact with twenty-six outlaw clubs during the years of 1969–1972 in the Cincinnati area alone.

The summer of 1972 was the end of this three-and-a-half-year ministry to the motorcycle gangs of Southern Ohio, Southern Indiana, and Northern Kentucky. Round, the figurehead of this subculture, was on parole and with his lack of leadership, due to the parole requirements, the Iron Horsemen ceased to exist. When the IH were no longer visible or heard of, other gangs began to drop from the scene. The image of the motorcycle gang member was no longer as attractive as it had been. The police made membership in a gang unattractive because of their intensity to hassle individual gang members, the public had reached a point where they would no longer tolerate the gangs, and sensing a loss of power in the gang presence, many citizens began to fight back to regain their neighborhoods.

I was also getting tired of taking the risks. I was tired of associating in a subculture with all the personalities of that environment. The ministry to the gangs was one of constantly giving to them, and being a bachelor father, I needed to give more to my two kids. I felt the need to reconnect more to a normal existence as pastor to a congregation, to immerse myself in my family, to no longer have sudden, violent, and surprising interruptions in my home and life. But, most important, I needed to spend time renewing the inner light and fire of my own spiritual being.

I don't know how many, if any, are around today. If there are some around, and I am sure there are, I wonder in which part of the country they are most prevalent.

The late 60s and early 70s seemed ripe for a guy to join an outlaw biker club. They had a great need to be wanted and be somebody, and the biker clubs took care of that need. The same needs exist in young people today, but they seem to have found other places to get that need fulfilled. It is not my intention to explain why because I don't know. But, when and if outlaw biker clubs become popular again, some other minister will have to enter the arena.

I have mentioned Round, the president of the Iron Horsemen often. I mentioned my specific goal was to reach the "biggest fish" in the subculture of the outlaw motorcycle world. Round was the undisputed leader of the biggest and baddest group of bikers. All the bikers of each club knew Round. The law enforcement officers from bordering states, several counties, cities, and towns knew him or knew of him. The newspaper and television reporters all knew him. Most of Cincinnati knew about him and the Iron Horsemen.

The Iron Horsemen colors consisted of a horse's head, with wing-like ears, a swastika for its eye, and a kind of sneering smile. Just like the fear one had of the Horsemen when they roared down the streets, the symbol also elicited an eerie feeling in those who saw it.

Round, a native Cincinnatian, attended St. Xavier and Purcell High Schools but didn't graduate. He was married and had two sons and a daughter.

He bought his first motorcycle when he was fourteen, "an old '45 army two-wheeler for fifteen dollars."

Round worked as an oxygen serviceman for a well-known firm, which sent him to West Virginia to go to school.

"That's where I became interested in riding a cycle. My boss got all warped out of shape. He told me to cut my hair and trim my moustache. And I did.

"Then he told me not to drive my bike to work, that I had to give up my bike. So, I told him where to stick his job and I walked out.

"Most of us have put just about all our savings, all our money, and all our lifetimes into the bikes and their ain't much room for anything else. Hell, the house of one of our club members was bombed and he wheeled out his motorcycle before he made sure his wife and kids were out."

Round was asked about the accusation by the police that the Iron Horsemen had stolen motorcycles and stripped them to sell the parts or use them on their own bikes.

He answered, "All I can say is if we do, our city police force is not very good. If they've got all that down and haven't caught us yet, shame on 'em."

Round's wife worked as a waitress and he hustled jobs for a few bucks when he needed the money. He tried going back to school when I first got to know him. He said he was getting tired of his teachers asking what he did for a living. He said it got bad when his kid's teachers began asking his kids what their dad did for a living. "I was more or less known as a criminal."

Round's first criminal conviction was when he was eighteen. He was arrested for stealing a battery. While president of the Iron Horsemen, he was convicted on three charges in the Hamilton County Common Pleas Court for receiving stolen goods. He was sentenced to three concurrent terms of one-to-seven years at the Ohio Reformatory at Mansfield. "Since then, my only conviction was for possession of a submachine gun. I got off in July 1972.

"The difference between us and an AMA club is that the AMA (American Motorcycle Association) bends over backward to meet society's demands. We are not a conformist group. We like to be individuals. I think we all recognize that we are different.

"None of us ever excelled in school, in athletics or in anything else. But together, we're one helluva team. That's the way it's always been. No Horseman is worth a damn without the others. We're a mechanized strike force that works perfect together and ain't worth a damn alone.

"I enjoy the bad image to a certain extent. But, it is a problem sometimes with citizens. A few years ago, a brother and I were riding along on our bikes when a couple of citizens jumped out of their car and ice-picked him a couple of times in the guts. I couldn't retaliate because I had to haul ass with my brother to the hospital.

"The other day a guy stuck a '45 (automatic weapon) out his car window and started shooting in the air. He decided to be cute, ya know? Trying to be a tough guy with a Horseman. Things like that happen.

"The way I handled it was to go over to his car and kick in his car door. We have to retaliate sometimes.

"The rednecks know damn sure not to run their mouths, especially to a Horseman. The citizens all know that if you're going to mess with one Horseman you're going to have to mess with all of them and you better be damned sure you can take all of them. We also have learned that the winner is not necessarily the one who fought a fair fight. Fair fight my ass. That is a lot of bull."

The Iron Horsemen was not the largest biker club, but it was by far the most violent, most feared, and the number one problem for the Cincinnati police. Round was the most prominent, influential, and powerful leader in the outlaw biker world of Southwestern Ohio, Southern Indiana, Northern Kentucky, and in the Midwest. When he got on his Harley with his Nazi helmet and Horsemen colors, there was no question who was in charge.

All the Horsemen respected him. Everyone feared him. In a newspaper interview he was asked, "How did you become the national president of the Iron Horsemen?"

He replied, "All the chapters got together and I walked in with two guys with guns and just said I was taking the damn thing over. I thought I was the guy for the job."

Seldom did he offer a handshake to anyone, but when he did it was accompanied by an attention getting, "Hey, man." His personality and engaging conversation made him a very likable person. Although he had an angry demeanor and negative outlook on life and was hard-nosed, there was something interesting about him that made people warm up to him and like him.

Whenever I was with the Horsemen when there was trouble and a crowd had gathered with a lot of police around, Round seemed to have the police loose and laughing. They all knew him and when they were called to a scene where the Iron Horsemen were the principle characters, they immediately took Round to the side to talk it over.

When I had weddings at the church in which the Iron Horsemen were involved, Round made sure no nonsense took place. Before one service, a Horseman was going to shoot off his gun outside the church as a signal that it was time for the service to start. Round grabbed the gun out of his hand and asked him, "What the hell you doin'?"

He told Round, "The preacher's got no bell and I wanted to get things started." Round put the gun in his belt and told him and the others to take a seat.

At another wedding which involved the Horsemen, with other clubs invited, people were gathering before the service and Hawk, a Satan's Angel, lit up some grass. Round walked over, grabbed it from him and put it out on his colors. "What the hell you doin'? We are at the preacher's church. We got something goin' on here. Pull anymore of this shit, and you and your brothers will be out of here."

One night I was at Round's house during a time when the Iron Horsemen were at war with the Dracos. Some Dracos rode up and down his street on their bikes waiting for someone, particularly Round, to come out of his house. I was very concerned because a few days before, the Dracos had shot a couple of windows out of the house of one of the Horsemen. Round and his wife would take an occasional look out the window to check out the activity. I was afraid to leave and grew more anxious as time went by. Round was watching television and talking to me as if nothing of significance was going on. When he thought it was okay for me to leave, he escorted me to my car with his shotgun cradled in his arm.

Round always knew what to say and how to say it. He never spoke without thinking about what he was going to say. When an issue or question would come up for discussion, several Horsemen made spontaneous off-the-cuff comments. Round would just be sitting there, quietly thinking. Then he would say what was going to happen. He was very decisive, absolute, and unwavering.

The biggest confrontation Round and the Iron Horsemen had was in another war with the Outlaws. This time it was with a chapter of the Outlaws from near Crawfordsville, Indiana. The Outlaws of that chapter made some remarks about the Horsemen not being strong enough to run the Midwest. They made insulting comments about the women of the Horsemen not being good enough for the Outlaws.

The clinching insult for the Horsemen was that one of the Indiana Outlaws had stolen a Horseman's bike. That was far worse than stealing colors. The Horsemen made the trip to Indiana in four cars, a van, and several bikes. Because of their enterprising ways, the Horsemen had gathered together some explosives, a bazooka, and other weapons to blow up the meeting place of the Outlaws and terrorize them.

After they did their business to the meeting place of the Outlaws, they returned to Cincinnati on I-74. Before they crossed the Indiana State Line, an Indiana State Trooper stopped the last car in the caravan because the car had a taillight out.

According to the Horsemen, he was not a very big trooper and they had the impression he was young and inexperienced. All the bikes and all the other cars in the caravan pulled over. They thought he seemed nervous as if it was his first time to stop a caravan of bikers out late at night. Round, who was riding one of the bikes at the front of the caravan, got off his bike as did all the other Horsemen. The Horsemen began to approach the trooper as he walked up to the front of the caravan. When they met, they made small talk, he gave them a warning, and told them to get the taillight fixed when they got back in town. All the eyes of the Horsemen were on the tropper as he walked past their cars back to his patrol car.

Out of the corner of his eye, the trooper noticed a bazooka in the back seat of one of the cars. The Horsemen said he froze in his tracks as if he had seen a dead body. When he got to his patrol car, they could tell he was calling for backup. The Horsemen knew better than to leave or do anything to cause more trouble than what was going to happen.

The result? Several were indicted and Round was sent to the Terra Haute federal penitentiary. Round was later released and became an informant for the FBI.

That experience took place in the early seventies and it ended the reign of Round as the president of the Iron Horsemen and started the decline of the Cincinnati chapter.

Jim Adams, the editor of the *Cincinnati Post and Times Star* who did the article about the Iron Horsemen which received so much review, said he saw Round in the foyer near the elevators of the *Cincinnati Post and Times Star* building just a few years ago. Jim said he looked like the same old Round he remembered from the days when the Horsemen terrorized Southwest Ohio and Northern Kentucky.

Round recognized Jim and told him, "My days are numbered, Mr. Adams. If you don't hear from me in two or three weeks, you can assume I am at the bottom of the Ohio River wearing concrete boots." Jim said he never heard from Round again.

CHAPTER ELEVEN

The church has a biblical imperative to become involved in ministry to the unchurched in its community. Each church should ask itself, "What is that special evangelical/mission task that we should be about?" Each year the church should evaluate that evangelical/mission task: "Have we accomplished our mission? If not, what is left to do? If so, what is our next opportunity? What area of our community needs to be penetrated, touched, helped, and made aware that Christ comes to offer a new life; that the church exists and is alive and caring?"

I was scheduled to speak at the Cherry Grove United Methodist Church in May of 1970. Jim Stewart was the pastor. Jim was a good friend of mine from seminary and was doing an excellent job as pastor of the Cherry Grove church. Prior to my coming to his church to speak he wrote, "We are looking forward to seeing you and hearing about the ministry you are conducting. I hope it might prompt our congregation to look at the ministry we can carry out in our community."

Every church must ask, "What is the ministry we can carry out in our community?"

The NUMC did not take the position of a spectator to outlaw motorcycle clubs. It became involved. Through its involvement and its participation in this mission and ministry to the bikers, some came to worship services and church activities, some received the sacrament of baptism, and some joined the church. When those outlaw bikers gathered and kneeled with the members of the church to receive communion, we all ceased being spectators in ministry. Each church has to judge for itself if it is just spectating or if it is a mission in its own backyard.

I did not know what goals to set when I began this ministry. I had no idea what to expect because I knew nothing about outlaw motorcycle clubs or outlaw motorcycle club members. The biker world was completely foreign to me. I never expected to get involved as deeply as I did and certainly not as quickly.

I had only a general idea of what I could do, and that was to get to know the Brothers In Arms. They were in my own backyard. I had no timetable to go by or a step-by-step procedure to do even that.

As I became involved with the BIA, I learned there were several other outlaw clubs in the Cincinnati area. I felt that I should make contact with them also, but again, I had no timetable or a specific way to go about it.

The goals were set with the help of the steering committee. Because we were all inexperienced, those goals were rather vague. The only real and specific goal I had was to reach out to and engage the very biggest and baddest of the outlaw bikers. That would have been Round and the Iron Horsemen. There were no guidelines or methods of setting goals for this kind of ministry.

Our discussion and planning centered on the intent and purpose for this ministry. Why even do it? What did we want to accomplish? The bottom line was that unless we acted and got involved, the outlaw biker world around Cincinnati, Northern Kentucky, and Southern Indiana would never be exposed to Christ. We hoped that, in time, this ministry would have some bikers dropping out of the clubs, getting jobs, returning to a life with their families, returning to school, and getting involved in the life of a church.

One Sunday in the last month of my ministry at Northside, Casey came into the sanctuary with his wife to attend worship. When I first saw them, I didn't recognize who he was. Then it dawned on me that it was Casey. He did not look like the tall, skinny kid I shoved away from a pledge he was beating. This guy had short hair and was wearing a suit and tie. The words of the hymn became blurred to me as I began to visualize all the encounters and experiences I had with him. In the blurred stanzas of the hymn, I saw this thug on his Harley chopper, Nazi helmet, and gloves with steel studs on each knuckle. Every time he would get stared at by citizens while on his bike, he would give the finger to them. When I would hang around the Iron Horsemen, he was one of the few who pointed a finger at me and threateningly told me, "Keep your distance from me, Preacher." He never forgave me for shoving him away from beating up that pledge before all his brothers. But here he was in worship. Before the hymn was over, I began to tear up and singing the hymn was difficult.

After the service, he introduced me to his wife. He said they stopped in to tell me goodbye. They were moving to her hometown of Indianapolis where he was going to work. I reached out to shake his hand but instead, he hugged me and told me, "Let's keep in touch, Skip."

Having former bikers call and ask me to visit a friend or family member who was in the hospital or needed a pastoral visit was especially meaningful. It meant that they trusted me, but that they also trusted in the One that drew me to them. I performed weddings of former bikers and their mamas. When an ex-biker called me to be their pastor in those ways, it was significant because it meant that they had been touched by Christ's love. It meant that, in some ways, the purpose of this ministry had been accomplished.

The real results can't be totally realized. Seeds were sown in so many ways; the ladies from the church who provided meals on Sundays when bikers stayed for dinner after worship and for the six drop-outs who stayed at the parsonage. The picture of J. Hook, the little old lady who needed a few bucks, the University of Illinois memorabilia which drew all kinds of comments, Jim Adams, Mr. Wilheit, the Lambings, the Hoppers, Alan North and his family, Paul Zentgraf, and little Mr. Whitekamp.

I never kept a log of statistics of the results of this ministry. One doesn't do that with the work of the Holy Spirit. I am just thankful to God for placing me in that place and time and giving me the opportunity to serve Him in that unique ministry. It was the most challenging and exciting experience of my life. I would have committed a serious error if I had I not been sensitive to what God was calling me to do, if I had not been tuned in to what role I could play. I thank God for helping me see those men as persons for whom the love of Christ was intended.

Would I do it again? As I look back and remember all I went through, my immediate response is "no." I don't know how I did it. But, then, in 1969, I had no choice. It was what God was calling me to do. He led me to respond to and accept the conviction that I was the right person at the right time in the right place to do His work.

Would I do it again? As I think about an answer to that question, I look back and see some of the things I got myself into, such as hassles with the police. A United Methodist minister getting whacked on the back of the helmet with a nightstick by one of Cincinnati's finest? I had never been in a fight in my life, and during that ministry I had to have my makeshift weapon just to go out at night. There were circumstances in which I had no choice but to hit people. I was around people and in an environment and circumstances that bred violence. Options were limited on what I could do and how to do it. In many cases, I didn't have the time to consider the consequences. I don't know what I would have done if I had been a Quaker. More often, though, I got punched, beaten, kicked, cut with bear bottles, cussed at, ridiculed, threatened, and pushed around by people I didn't even know.

Would I do it again? I have to think of my kids and their response to that question. They both look back on those years at Northside with fond memories. They were treated by those outlaw bikers with gentleness, love, and care. The best babysitters I had were guys who were armed, had jail records, did not come from a wholesome home, were street-wise, dirty, and knew violence as a way of life. Away from my kids they fought with brass knuckles and chain belts, terrorized people, destroyed property, were thieves, and had no family but their brothers.

But they discovered with us and within the walls of our home and the people of the Northside United Methodist Church that they had a very special family. They were accepted and loved. They did not have to be on guard all the time. They found that being trusted was empowering and made them feel redeemed. They came to know and respect boundaries of right from wrong. Some of them carried that newfound experience into the street and their biker world. They became less prone to spontaneous reaction and violence. They thought before they acted. I saw Tony, of the Brothers In Arms, let a little old lady take a place in line in front of him at a convenience store. Since I was with him that night, that might have made a difference in his behavior. But I have been with them when they pushed people aside and made complete jerks of themselves.

In return for the time and effort the Skipworth family gave, we felt protected, accepted, loved, and trusted. We began to experience courtesy, thoughtfulness, and a quiet demeanor as they spent more and more time with us. After a while, they began to freeload less and began to bring in groceries and treats. Yale and Nancy never lacked for toys or sweet treats or attention or someone to join them watching cartoons.

Would I do it again? My answer takes into account the struggle it took to gain the trust that I needed to develop with the bikers. I think of the extra money and time it took from my family. I take into account the fear I felt each time I was out in public with those guys. The only time people knew I was a minister was when I wore my collar. Most of the time I didn't wear it and some redneck would want to get a piece of me, thinking I was a member of the Henchmen or Devil's Disciples. It happened at a bar in Norwood. A half-drunk good ol' boy said, "Whose the fairy lookin' greaser with no colors? All you cycle-trash get the hell out of here and take him with you. What ya think this is, a fruit-bar?"

If I told them, "I am just riding with these guys; I am a really a United Methodist minister," not only would they have had a big laugh, they also would have thrown me right through the front door.

In order to protect me, Deuce just told everybody there, "We are going to leave. We didn't come here to cause a hassle."

I often wondered what would have happened if I had not been with them that night. They would have stayed and fought and then I would have been called to go to the hospital to "pick up the pieces of the Devil's." I told Deuce, "Like it or not, I saved your skins tonight."

Deuce shot back, "That's a hell of a lot easier than saving our souls."

Would I do it again? I consider, of most importance, my own personal spiritual growth and faith development from this experience. As we grow older as Christians, we need to search for and be open to see and accept new and different opportunities and challenges that God may place before us. We need to tempt our sense of adventure. As we grow older, we also need to be ready to develop new interests and abilities. We don't grow if we don't allow new challenges to come into our lives. I am grateful to God for placing this challenge before me in the time and place that it happened.

Would I do it again? Yes, because I had to keep a promise I made to God in June of 1947. For a year, the Skipworth's were living in Southern Illinois in the oil fields near New Haven. I had just completed the fifth grade. Before moving to the oil fields around New Haven, my dad worked in the oil fields near St. Elmo where I grew up and went to grade school. I did not like the New Haven oil leases where dad worked. I went to a one room school, the teacher was mean, I had no friends, the kids looked down on us (they called us "oil field trash"), and we lived out in the country in an old dilapidated farm house near the oil lease. I wanted so much to move back to St. Elmo.

In June of 1947, we were driving back to St. Elmo to visit and dad was going to look into a job in the oil fields there. As we drove back on Route 45 to St. Elmo, I was sitting in the back seat of our 1936 Ford with my younger brother, Frank. I have remembered all my life the prayer I prayed to God. "God, if you will let daddy get a job back in St. Elmo, I will do anything you want me to do." Daddy got the job and we moved back to St. Elmo. I kept my promise. Ministering to the gangs was a part of that promise.

I don't ask the question anymore, "Would I do it again?" I ask, "What is it now that He calls me to do? What is it now that He expects of me? What new opportunity is before me to serve Him?"

The biblical imperative is that God calls us to breathe new life into the despairing lives of others, to breathe the breath of hope into those who only feel hopelessness, to breathe the breath of trust into those who don't feel they are trusted or that they can trust others. To breathe the power of faith into a spirit that has no faith, to breathe His love into the lives of those who don't feel loved.

During the Babylonian exile, God spoke to Ezekiel to breathe new life and hope into the people of Israel. As Ezekiel walked the Valley of the Dry Bones, he saw in the bones the despair and hopelessness of his people. The bones exemplified the need for change, for new life, for hope. In the bones, he saw that the people no longer knew God or had a sense of self-worth.

God grabbed me. God's Spirit took me up and set me down in the middle of an open plain strewn with bones. He led me around and among them—a lot of bones! There were bones all over the plain—dry bones, bleached by the sun.

He said to me, "Son of man, can these bones live?"

I said, "Master God, only you know that."

He said to me, "Prophesy over these bones: 'Dry bones, listen to the Message of God!'"

God, the Master, told the dry bones, "Watch this: I'm bringing the breath of life to you and you'll come to life. I'll attach sinews to you, put meat on your bones, cover you with skin, and breathe life into you. You'll come alive and you'll realize that I am God!"

I prophesied just as I'd been commanded. As I prophesied, there was a sound and, oh, rustling! The bones moved and came together, bone to bone. I kept watching. Sinews formed, then muscles on the bones, then skin stretched over them. But they had no breath in them.

He said to me, "Prophesy to the breath. Prophesy, son of man. Tell the breath, 'God, the Master, says, Come from the four winds. Come, breath. Breathe on these slain bodies. Breathe life!'"

So I prophesied, just as he commanded me. The breath entered them and they came alive! They stood up on their feet, a huge army.

Then God said to me, "Son of man, these bones are the whole house of Israel. Listen to what they're saying: 'Our bones are dried up, our hope is gone, there's nothing left of us.'

"Therefore, prophesy. Tell them, 'God, the Master, says: I'll dig up your graves and bring you out alive—O my people! Then I'll take you straight to the land of Israel. When I dig up graves and bring you out as my people, you'll realize that I am God.

I'll breathe my life into you and you'll live. Then I'll lead you straight back to your land and you'll realize that I am God. I've said it and I'll do it. God's Decree'" (Eze. 37:1–14 THE MESSAGE).

I have mentioned some of the bikers who changed, who came to have an infusion of God's spirit. They went from a hardened, jaded, insensitive, and calloused view of life to one which had undergone a transformation. But, there were so many others who were like the strewn dry bones over the plain. Where are they now? What happened to them? Did they make it? Did they ever have the breath of God's spirit enter their lives?

What about the drunken pledges that gathered along the river bank challenging each other to a fight? What about the guy who broke the beer bottle against the wall at the Black Dome and was going to cut me up with it? Did Little Jesus ever hear or see or experience the breath of God? What about Cowboy, the Gladiator, who was going to bash my brains in with a beer bottle as my back was turned to him? Did he just end up as one of the dry bones?

I encountered twenty-six different outlaw biker clubs. Each club had about fifteen members. That would be almost four hundred bikers. As Ezekiel said, "Those are a lot of bones." A lot of young men who needed to have the breath of God breathed into their souls, minds, and bodies.

I don't know what happened to Round, or Farmer John, or Cutter, or Crazy Horse, or so many others. I only hope that the spirit of God found them and breathed new life, joy, and love into them.

I have mentioned those who did "come back," who did come "alive" as if God breathed his spirit into them. When I think of them, I think it was all worthwhile.

POSTSCRIPT

As I struggled home after being beaten by two motorcycle gangs at the Northside Teen Association dance, I asked the question, "What am I doing here?" When the Brothers In Arms came into my home for the first time and I saw their weapons, I asked, "What have I gotten myself into?" During the three years of ministering to the Henchmen, Cobras, Devil's Disciples, Satan Sinners, Coffin Cheaters, Iron Horsemen, and twenty other outlaw motorcycle clubs, I often asked, "Why am I doing this?" What did I accomplish in all this? So many times I was afraid, and did not know what to do or what to say. Did any good come out of this? Did I make a difference in the lives of any of these men?

Of all the tests and precarious predicaments I encountered, the worst was being placed in the middle of the Butler County sheriff's department and the Iron Horsemen.

One of the Horsemen had raped and killed a young twenty year old lady. It was a gruesome murder. He dismembered her body and left a horrific mess at the scene of the crime. It did not take long for him to be apprehended. His mother, seeing him come in late at night covered with blood, called the police. Since the crime occurred in Butler County, he was taken to the county jail there.

Round and several Iron Horsemen called me and wanted me to go with them to the jail. Round told me, "We've got a brother, Face, in serious trouble and we need you to go see him. Wear your collar. It's going to take all we got for the Horsemen to make it through this one. We can't visit him, but you can."

We arrived in two cars. No bikes were ridden this time. I don't know why. Maybe since this crime had been the worst I had ever encountered with the Horsemen and the worst they had experienced in their own brotherhood, it had a settling effect on them. It might have been they did not want to push too far by riding up on Harleys as outlaws coming back to the scene of the crime. Or, maybe the Horsemen didn't want the sound of all those Harleys intruding on a very serious and somber occasion in the community and thus giving the wrong impression to people. Maybe it was such a heinous crime they knew the public had reached its threshold of tolerance with outlaw bikers, especially them, and visibility on bikes would have created an open-season. Maybe it was out of respect for the circumstances that surrounded why they were there.

When we entered the sheriff's building and jail, Round introduced me to one of the sheriff's staff as their preacher and told him I came to see Face. A sheriff's deputy took me upstairs to see Face. Face knew who I was. I had been with him on several occasions with the IH. He was a good-looking young man, very quiet. He seemed to be on the periphery of the activities of the Iron Horsemen most of the time. I imagined he was one of the dropouts from high school who was a nobody until he joined the Horsemen. I never knew him to be one to fight or cause trouble with anyone. He was never loud. He was always cordial and welcoming to me.

I waited in the visitor's room while the deputy went to get Face. When he came into the room, he sat across from me behind the bars of the visitor's window. Face gave me the impression he could not understand why I was there. He seemed surprised. He looked bewildered. It was as if he was saying, "I didn't do anything wrong. I sure don't need a preacher here. This is not the last rites. I don't see any reason why a preacher should be here."

He started off with the usual hard line. "I didn't invite you here, preacher." Then he got into a nonchalant attitude which I thought was to mask his fear and the confusion he must have felt. In spite of his tough role-playing, I felt he was sensitive to his predicament.

Face wanted to know if Round came with me. I told him yes. I told him that eleven of his brothers were downstairs, but they couldn't visit him—only I could. He asked if Crazy Horse, Farmer John, and Scarface were there. I told him yes.

From then on the only question he asked was whether I had talked to his mom. Without my answering him, he told me to go see her and make sure she was OK. He said, "I know she is having a hard time. I have given her nothing but grief all my life. And now, this. Promise me you will go see her, preacher."

I promised him I would visit his mother. I asked, "Is there anything you want me to tell her?"

"Tell her everything will be OK."

I stayed with him a few minutes. I asked him if he needed anything. He shook his head no. When the deputy motioned to me that it was getting time to leave, I asked Face if he would mind if I prayed with him. He didn't respond one way or the other. I slowly reached out under the bars and placed my hand on his. He didn't look up to my face but I noticed a tear coming down his right cheek. A tear was forming in the corner of his other eye. He lowered his head and sobbed. He wouldn't look up at me. He didn't say a word. I held his hand and we waited for a moment in total quiet. I looked up at the deputy and he simply nodded. I bowed to pray. I didn't know what to pray or even if I could pray. I just held his hand and waited.

Although he was not tried and convicted, I knew I was holding the hand of a rapist, a murderer, and the soul of an empty and struggling young man. In the quiet of that moment, I prayed a prayer I had used often in so many terrible circumstances. "Father God, Good Shepherd over all of us, place your shepherding care on Face. Let him feel your hands of love on his shoulders. Lift him up with your arms into your forgiveness, your love, and your grace. Through Jesus, your Son, make him whole. Amen." The deputy walked over, placed his hand on Face's shoulder, and Face let go of my hand. I went downstairs where the Horsemen were waiting.

On the way to Hamilton, I was in the first car—driven by Bull—and was sitting in the back seat by the door. On the ride back to Cincinnati, I began to suspect something that made me a bit fearful. I felt some anxiety because I was sitting in the middle of the front seat between Round and Scarface. Round was driving. I didn't expect to hear what Round said to me.

Round said, "The cops told us you told them that Face confessed to you." He didn't look at me after he said it. He just stared straight ahead at the road. He didn't say anything else. He just drove the car. No one in the car said anything.

I told Round that the cops didn't talk to me and I didn't talk to them. I didn't say anything else. I felt helpless. I was now being used by the cops. I was being put in the middle again, only this time, it was not between two gangs at war, or two bikers ready to fight, but between the police and the Iron Horsemen.

Round said, "That's not what we heard. We heard you gave him away."

I was scared. I was stuck between two monster men who, if they believed the police, would do away with me without a thought. I prayed that they would consider and honor the years I had spent with them as pastor, confessor, and reconciler. I prayed that they would hold fast my role with them as a conduit to hope, peace, and the love of Christ.

The ride back to Cincinnati got longer and slower. I expected the car to stop anytime. I expected the car doors to open; the five Horsemen and the ones in the car behind us pull me out, beat me, and leave me for dead. We kept driving. Farmer John was sitting in the back seat, and put his heavy hands on my shoulders. I froze in fear of what was coming next. Farmer John said, "We know better, preacher."